D0907471

Faith and the Intellectual Life

Faith
and the
Intellectual Life

Marianist Award Lectures

EDITED BY

James L. Heft, S.M.

University of Notre Dame Press
Notre Dame and London

© 1996 by
University of Notre Dame Press
Notre Dame, Indiana 46556
All Rights Reserved

Manufactured in the United States of America

Library of Congress Cataloging-in-Publication Data

Faith and the intellectual life.
    p.   cm.
Lectures presented by recipients of the Marianist Award.
Includes bibliographical references.
ISBN 0-268-00994-5 (alk. paper)
    1. Catholics—United States—Intellectual life. 2. Catholic
learning and scholarship.
BX1407.I5F35   1996
282'.73'0904—dc20   95-50809
                                                          CIP

The paper used in this publication meets the minimum requirements
of the American National Standard for Information Sciences—
Permanence of Paper for Printed Library Materials, ANSI Z39.48-1984.

Dedicated to Brother Stanley G. Mathews, S.M.,
Rector of the University of Dayton, 1982–1983,
for his leadership, service, and wisdom

Contents

vii

Preface:

Loving God With Your Mind and Your Heart

Since 1986, the University of Dayton has presented the Marianist Award to a Roman Catholic distinguished for intellectual achievement. The recipients of the Award over the past decade include not only theologians, but also historians, a mathematician, a legal scholar, a psychologist, a philosopher of religion, a political scientist, and a—well, how does one "categorize" the multi-faceted scholarly work of polymath Walter Ong?

The Award was originally presented, beginning in 1950, the Marian Year, to individuals who had made outstanding contributions to Mariology. Seven years before, in 1943, the University had established the Marian Library, the holdings of which are now known throughout the world. To make even greater use of these holdings, the International Marian Research Institute was founded in 1975, in affiliation with the Pontifical Theological faculty Marianum in Rome, through which Licentiate and Doctoral degrees are awarded. Even though more Marian research than ever has been undertaken at the University in recent years, in 1986 the focus of the Marianist Award was changed from Marian scholarship to distinguished scholarship by a Roman Catholic.

The recipient of the Award is invited to the University in January, when the Marianists commemorate the death of their founder, William Joseph Chaminade (1761–1850). The Society of Mary, founded in Bordeaux, France in 1817, is a religious community of 1,700 brothers and priests located throughout Europe, North and South America, Africa and India. The Marianists draw their spirituality from the ample resources of the French School out of which Fr. Chaminade fashioned an action-oriented Marian spirituality that encourages the integration of head and heart; that is, the development of an intellectual life shaped by what Chaminade called the faith of the heart. The emphasis on community also draws strength from the Marianist's unique composition: brothers and priests who live together, without distinction or privilege, and serve others. In terms of the intellectual life, Marianists stress learning in communities where collaboration and service help to keep reflection loving, and love thoughtful.

The recipients of the Marianist Award are invited to reflect upon how their personal faith has influenced their scholarship. In the academy today, these two dimensions—religious faith and scholarship—often occupy two different compartments, hermetically sealed off from each other, so as to prevent the alleged distortion of objective scholarship by subjective faith. As numerous recent studies have made clear, however, scholarship, even in the sciences, inescapably incorporates personal elements, and faith can provide a deeper understanding without distorting what one studies. In Catholic universities, no split between personal faith and the intellectual life ought to exist. In Catholic universities, the love of learning and the desire for God, to borrow the title of a 1950's classic by the Benedictine Jean Leclercq, ought to be blended with neither confusion nor embarrassment.

Hence, the Marianist Award, as redefined in 1986, emphasizes the importance of that balance between learning and love, that consonance of the head and the heart. The recipients of this Award typically meet the University community before and after their lecture in classrooms, at receptions and around a dinner table. In all these places, both faith and the intellectual life are strengthened.

The lectures contained in this volume give eloquent witness to lives of faith and intelligence. The first recipient of the Award, the late John Tracy Ellis, revises his earlier criticism of Catholic higher education, made in his famous 1955 lecture on "American Catholics and Intellectual Life." While once he thought that Catholic colleges and universities stressed the moral and formative dimensions of education to the detriment of the intellectual, in his 1986 Marianist Award lecture he argues for the preservation of the former to balance and complement the latter. The next year's Award recipient, Rosemary Haughton, blends in her autobiographical reflection a deep love for the Church and a searing criticism of its shortcomings. Similarly, Timothy O'Meara calls for a greater rapport between science and religion, and a closer relationship between the founding religious orders of Catholic universities and the laity who already have been called upon to lead such institutions. Walter Ong describes in expansive and inclusive strokes the nature of Catholicism and the importance of Catholic scholarship today.

The 1990 recipient, Sidney Callahan, explains the extraordinary intellectual riches she discovered in Catholicism when she entered the Church as a student at Bryn Mawr. The personal impact of the Second Vatican Council, especially the debates during the Council, the historical evolution of certain moral doctrines and the realization that Scripture was shaped by the context of a particular community—all these experiences led John T. Noonan to realize more clearly than ever before that Catholic Christianity presumes a humanism by and through which God acts.

The following year's lecturer, Yale philosopher of religion, Louis Dupré, focuses on the joys and responsibilities of being a Catholic teacher, a vocation made all the more challenging in our own age with "its unprecedented refusal to accept any restrictions to raw individualism, its general decline of civility, honesty, and respect for life—human and planetary—a period of moral bankruptcy." In 1993's lecture, Monika Hellwig of Georgetown University traces her personal journey from war-torn Europe to the United States, highlighting the different shapes of Catholicism in each of these parts of the world and the challenge of being a Catholic theologian today.

Philip Gleason, a 1951 graduate of the University of Dayton, describes how the Catholic Church in the United States has arrived at the point where, after 40 years of extensive change, its very identity has become a problem. And finally, in 1995, Bryan Hehir situates the Catholic Church in the midst of a rapidly changing world order, within which, mindful of its rich spiritual and intellectual heritage, the Church should minister with "confident modesty."

These lectures were given by a group of scholars committed to joining their personal faith to their intellectual life. In them, faith and intelligence constantly interact. Each of the recipients of the Marianist Award—philosopher, psychologist, legal scholar, theologian, historian or political scientist—provides us with a rich entreé to the Catholic intellectual tradition.

Finally, I wish to acknowledge the help of Mary A. Neacy, Executive Assistant to the President, who made sure not only that printable texts were available from the recipients of the Marianist Award, but also that hospitality and special arrangements made their visits such a pleasure for the University of Dayton community.

James L. Heft, S.M.
Provost
University of Dayton
Feast of St. Luke
October 18, 1995

Moral Values in Higher Education

JOHN TRACY ELLIS

We have undertaken the work; let us continue; I have never yet abandoned an enterprise once started, and I do not intend to begin now at my advanced age.[1]

These words were spoken by William Joseph Chaminade, founder of the Society of Mary, in 1823 in the face of grave financial difficulties that had overtaken the young Society by reason of his purchase of the Chateau of Saint-Remy, an undertaking that ultimately became "one of the most prosperous houses of the Society,"[2] in the judgment of a Marianist historian. I like to think of that brave stance of Father Chaminade as representative of the spirit that has carried this religious community through many a trial during the 170 years they have served the Church both in this country and in many foreign lands. Indeed, the problem that arose over the Chateau of Saint-Remy was minimal for a man who had, in defense of moral principle, refused to take the oath to the Civil Constitution of the Clergy demanded by France's revolutionary government, encountered the savagery of the Reign of Terror, and the rigors of exile at Saragossa in Spain. Nor did the misunderstanding with Jean de Cheverus, former Bishop of Boston and after 1826 Archbishop of Bordeaux, discourage Chaminade from pursuing what he viewed as his mission for the betterment of his fellow human beings.

Having paid that richly deserved tribute to the founder of the Society that brought this institution into being in the year that Father Chaminade went to God, my first words must be addressed to Brother Fitz, his confrères and lay colleagues for the honor they have done me with the Marianist Award of 1986. I do wish you all to know that I appreciate this generous action.

The year 1850 has more than a passing interest for those of you who compose this academic community. It was on July 1 of that year that what was initially called Saint Mary's School for Boys opened its doors to receive its original contingent of fourteen day students. Father Leo Meyer and his little band of Marianist Brothers would that day have been unaware that less than three weeks later the diocese in which they made their start would be raised by the Holy See to the rank of the Archdiocese of Cincinnati, and had they known it, it would doubtless have meant little to them. Nor would they have been much engaged in the heated national debate of that year that witnessed Henry Clay's compromise on the burning issue of the extension of slavery in which Clay, John C. Calhoun, Daniel Webster, and William H. Seward roused Americans, both North and South, in stirring orations that sought a compromise that ultimately failed to avert civil conflict. If these Marianists would have paused at the death of President Zachary Taylor a week after the opening of their school here in Dayton, they would have been less concerned when 1850 saw the birth of *Harper's Monthly Magazine*, the arrival of the Swedish 'nightingale,' Jenny Lind, and least of all by the importation of the Brooklyn Institute of eight pairs of English sparrows to protect shade trees from the damaging caterpillars!

These pioneer Marianists were part of an immense throng of Catholic immigrants who numbered over 700,000 during the previous decade, bringing the Catholic population of the United States to 1,606,000 by 1850, attaining in that year the status of the largest religious denomination in the nation, a rank that the Catholics have held to the present day.

If Father Chaminade would have known of the expansion of his religious family to the United States before his death 136 years ago today, he would not have lived to hear of their first foundation here in Dayton. That Saint Mary's School for Boys bore little resemblance to the present flourishing University of Dayton is evident on many counts, for example, in the costs of attendance announced in the prospectus published in the *Catholic Telegraph* of Cincinnati to the effect that board and tuition, payable in advance, would be $18.00 per quarter, while day students would be charged $3.00 per quarter, figures that parents and student sponsors of 1986 would probably read with stark astonishment mingled with a touch of envy! And local ecumenists would today be less than amused at learning that Archbishop John B. Purcell approved the prospectus in his weekly newspaper, but added, "None but Catholic boys are admitted."[3]

When I accepted Brother Fitz's gracious invitation several months ago I asked myself what I could possibly say that would have any originality and relevance for an audience of this kind. Each week I read *The Chronicle of Higher Education* and find myself increasingly awed by the number and complexity of the problems that face American colleges and universities, especially those in the private sector. Having had little or no experience in educational administration, it would be presumption in a high degree for me to direct my remarks to any phase of that daunting area, an area that remains to me in good measure a *terra incognita.* The three-day conference held some months ago at the Wingspread Conference Center in Racine, Wisconsin, in an effort to reform undergraduate instruction is only one of the more recent examples of the baffling and intricate nature of higher education's problems,[4] and many more examples could easily be cited.

What, then, I asked myself, should be the central theme of this address? I concluded that since the University of Dayton is an institution with a clear and distinct religious affiliation, and that it finds itself along with all its sister institutions in a society where extreme individualism has taken a severe toll on national morale, it might not be out of place to speak about the importance of values, that is, moral values, and the responsibility that institutions of higher learning have to cultivate respect for such. In that regard what was said in the recent work of Cardinal Basil Hume, O.S.B., Archbishop of Westminster, concerning values in relation to politics can, I think, *mutatis mutandis,* be applied to education. "Value-systems," the cardinal declared:

as well as moral and ethical considerations must obviously have a bearing on politics, understood in this wider sense. It is simply impossible to create a community and regulate the lives and activities of its members in ways which are 'value-free.'[5]

Obviously, one cannot and should not expect that this or any other university of the 1980's should view this obligation with the simplicity that William Chaminade strove to inculcate among his relatively unlettered followers a century or more ago. Our sophisticated age demands a much more refined and nuanced approach if the effort is to prove effective. Yet for a university such as this to remain indifferent to values of this kind would be to betray its true character, and thus contribute indirectly to the disarray that has overtaken the lives of so many Americans of our time as portrayed, for example, by Christopher Lasch in *The Culture of Narcissism* (1978), and a year ago by Robert Bellah and his coauthors in *Habits of the Heart: Individualism and Commitment in American Life*, to cite only two among numerous analyses of the current scene.

I entertain no doubt, however, about the sense of responsibility in these matters that obtains in this institution, since I take it for granted that the University of Dayton affords an atmosphere in which personal integrity is given a high premium and is exemplified in the lives of the sons of Chaminade and their lay colleagues. Indeed, in this or any other academic community that duty can find no more effective channel or instrument than in the lives of the men and women who compose its faculty. As in so many other aspects of human conduct, Cardinal Newman phrased the point in a telling way that I have frequently quoted when he asked how truth had been sustained through the centuries in the face of such formidable obstacles and enemies, a question to which he replied:

> I answer that it has been upheld in the world not as a system, not by books, not by argument, nor by temporal power, but by the personal influence of such men as . . . are at once the teachers and patterns of it.[6]

To be the teachers and patterns of truth, it seems to me, is to fulfill an obligation of paramount importance for those who aspire to fashion and enrich the minds of the young. To be sure, to say this is to state an obvious fact known since the beginning of recorded history, a fact that will endure to the end of time. Yet I believe it warrants being heard again and again in an age such as our own that appears to be peculiarly bedeviled by a glaring disregard for honesty and truthfulness. Disregard or indifference to these fundamental concepts inevitably breeds distrust and suspicion and tends to poison human relations on every level from that of the super-powers juggling for advantage over each other down to the lowest plane of social contact where pervasive thievery, lying, and deceit have gravely corroded the trust and confidence that must obtain if humankind is to conduct its day-to-day affairs on anything suggesting a mutually helpful basis.

In a society that would appear to have found an increasing patronage for the philosophy of 'looking out for number one,' and in which individualism has been carried to an excessive degree by all too many, the likelihood of success in cultivating restraint is seriously diminished. Yet the effort cannot be abandoned lest American youth be even further cut adrift from the moorings that offer them a prospect of stability and a meaningful existence. In a world of ceaseless and bewildering change there are certain things that remain the same. Among these unchanging factors is the human tendency to go to excess, to invoke liberty to the point that it becomes license, to indulge individual appetite for wealth, for power, and for sensual gratification to a degree that the common good is threatened and society itself is put at peril. If we of 1986 have been the startled witnesses, and some of our contemporaries the abused and wounded victims of actions springing from thinking of this kind, it is nothing especially new, save in the technological discoveries that have been employed to increase its menace. Nearly 200 years ago a discerning analysis of the phenomenon of unbridled individualism was expressed by Edmund Burke in a letter to a member of revolutionary France's National Assembly. "Men are qualified for civil liberty," said Burke

in exact proportion to their disposition to put moral chains upon their own appetites—in proportion as their love of justice is above their rapacity,—in proportion as their soundness and sobriety of understanding is above their vanity and presumption,—in proportion as they are disposed to listen to the counsels of the wise and the good, in preference to the flattery of knaves. Society cannot exist unless a controlling power upon will and appetite be placed somewhere; and the less of it there is within, the more there is without. It is ordained in the eternal constitution of things, that men of intemperate minds cannot be free. Their passions forge their fetters.[7]

Personally, I have never found a better summary of the matter than that contained in this oft-quoted letter of Edmund Burke. Its message has lost none of its force since it was written in 1791, a message that has a special value for this generation of humankind of the closing years of the twentieth century, a people harassed over the entire globe by violence of every description.

I do not wish to continue in this somber vein and thus cast a gloomy shadow over this joyous occasion. Yet to speak of moral values in the present context can scarcely be thought irrelevant, for most of those present at this academic convocation have as their principal goal in life the instruction and enlightenment of a future generation, a generation of youth which for the first time in American history has found life itself so confusing and without ultimate purpose that among their kind suicide is now second to accidents in taking the lives of the American young. If we of an older generation are, however, painfully conscious of society's ills and often feel powerless to effect a remedy, we should not permit the temptation to despair to paralyze our efforts. Here history can prove of strong support in furnishing evidence that the human family has frequently found itself in far worse circumstances than we are now experiencing. As the distinguished English historian, Sir Owen Chadwick, has said, "History . . . does more than any other discipline to free the mind from the tyranny of present opinion."[8] And if one has any doubt about that type of tyranny they need only advert to the menacing influence exercised among both the young and their elders by what is today called peer pressure.

History likewise bears testimony to the virtually inexhaustible resilience of the human spirit, for example, in the nation's story by its recovery from the crippling effects of the Civil War and the aftermath of the stock market crash of 1929 that left hardly a citizen of the Republic untouched by the unprecedented suffering that followed in its wake. On another level who should know better the lessons that history can teach in this regard than the members of the Society of Mary and their lay collaborators who belong to a Church with the longest and most eventful history of any ecclesiastical community? Even a superficial acquaintance with the Church's past testifies to her extraordinary ability to overcome obstacles of every description and, literally, to rise phoenix-like from seeming death to live and flourish once again. To cite a single example, in 1797 conditions of the Church in Chaminade's Bordeaux, and in France generally, rendered ecclesiastical life to the point of seeming extinction, a situation that sent the Marianists' founder and many others into exile in Spain, with little hope at the time of a return. Yet return he did in 1800 and seventeen years later launched this religious community as part of one of the most refulgent spiritual revivals that the modern Church has ever experienced.

That is the kind of heritage that the Dayton Marianists and their lay colleagues have to draw upon. You have, I am sure, made yourselves aware of the acute problems that must engage every person involved in higher education in what *Academe: Bulletin of the American Association of University Professors* in its issue of last October called, "This year of self-scrutiny," in allusion to reports such as "Reclaim a Legacy" of William J. Bennett, Secretary of Education, "Involvement in Learning," "Integrity in the College Curriculum," and the Bowen-Schuster study on the present condition and future prospect of college and university professors. In this regard the University of Dayton's faculty and administrators will seek the wisdom that is embodied in their heritage, but they will have the good judgment not to lean solely on the past, but rather to bring themselves abreast of the most perceptive and creative thinking of the present. A too great reliance on the one would be to cultivate an antiquarianism that would offer sterile results; to rely exclusively on each passing fad of the 1980's would be to trivialize the grave responsibility which each of you has assumed. In a word, you will have the good sense to blend the two and thus subscribe to the judgment expressed a half century ago by the famous Jesuit scientist, Pierre Teilhard de Chardin, when he wrote:

> The past has revealed to me how the future is built and preoccupation with the future tends to sweep everything else aside. It is precisely that I may be able to speak with authority about the future that it is essential for me to establish myself more firmly then before as a specialist on the past.[9]

With, then, a happy blending of the past and the present there ensues the wisdom with which to chart the future, to be sure, a daunting task for every university, yet one that every conscientious faculty will endeavor to fulfill in a way that will redound to the maximum benefit of their institution, and that means in a quite particular way to the students, the heralds of the future in any house of higher learning. If the University of Dayton may not have achieved the basketball fame of its sister institution in Honolulu,[10] it will, I sincerely hope and trust, continue to prosper in the more enduing achievement of cultivation of the things of the mind, and that with at least a suggestion of the no-nonsense attitude that brought this institution into being in 1850 when its prospectus read, "The Scholastic Year will open the first Tuesday of September and will be finished the last Tuesday in July. . . ."[11] No 'spring recess' in those days!

In closing permit me to renew my expression of gratitude for the honor you have done me this evening, and to wish for each of you—faculty, administrators, and students—a sense of personal gratification as you make your pilgrim way through the time ahead so that each of you may be able to say of his and her individual endeavor what Cardinal Newman expressed at the close of an exacting task that was brought off with signal success:

> Under these circumstances, then, what can I desire and pray for but this?—that what I have said well may be blest to those who have heard it, and that what I might have said better, may be blest to me by increasing my dissatisfaction with myself; that I may cheerfully resign myself to such trouble or anxiety as necessarily befalls anyone who has spoken boldly on an unpopular subject in a difficult time, with the confidence that no trouble or

anxiety but will bring some real good with it in the event, to those who have acted in sincerity, and by no unworthy methods, and with no selfish aim.[12]

Notes

1. John E. Gavin, S.M., *The Centenary of the Society of Mary.* Dayton: Mount Saint John. 1917. p. 76.

2. *Ibid.*

3. *Ibid.,* p. 174.

4. *The Chronicle of Higher Education,* XXXI (October 9, 1985), 24.

5. Basil Hume, C.S.B., *To Be A Pilgrim.* San Francisco: Harper & Row, Publishers. 1984. p. 163.

6. John Henry Newman, "Personal Influence, the Means of Propagating the Truth," *Fifteen Sermons Preached before the University of Oxford.* New York: Longmans, Green and Company. 1896. pp. 91–92.

7. Edmund Burke to a Member of the National Assembly of France, January 19, 1791. *The Writings and Speeches of Edmund Burke.* Boston: Little, Brown and Company. 1901. IV, 51–52.

8. Owen Chadwick, *Freedom and the Historian. An Inaugural Lecture.* Cambridge: At the University Press. 1969. p. 39.

9. Notes jotted down aboard the *Cathy* bound for Bombay, September 8, 1935, Bernard Wall (Ed.), *Letters from a Traveler.* New York: Harper & Brothers. 1956. pp. 207–208.

10. Charles Ferrell, "Hawaii's Tiny Chaminade U. Has a Part-Time Coach, No Gym, and a Record of Upsetting Top-Ranked Teams," *The Chronicle of Higher Education,* XXXI (January 8, 1986), 29–31.

11. Gavin, *op. cit.,* p. 174.

12. John Henry Newman, *Lectures on the Present Position of Catholics in England.* New York: Loggmans, Green and Company. 1903. p. 403.

Re-Discovering Church

ROSEMARY HAUGHTON

It is an unusual privilege for me to be able to make a presentation at which the subject is for me to decide, and which therefore gives me the opportunity to develop ideas which particularly interest me at the moment. There is an ancient story about the person who said "How do I know what I think until I hear what I say?", and most people find this funny because people are supposed to think first and speak afterwards. But people like myself who lecture or write don't really find it funny, but rather a realistic expression of the fact that for many of us it is the act of writing, or speaking out loud, that actually pulls together inchoate ideas, bits of information, and random intuitions, and gives them a coherence that deserves to be described as thought. That is why I welcomed this opportunity to try to discover what I think, as a Catholic in the eighties, standing at my own particular center of varied experiences—personal, ecclesial and global—at this point in my life.

New Self-Awareness of Catholicism

The invitation to receive this award mentioned that my past work has brought together dogma and spirituality in a practical way—that I believe that lived theology emerges from prayer, faith and community, and that I treasure the Catholic tradition.

It is true that I have done, or tried to do, these things. And it is in trying to do these things that I have found myself being forced constantly to re-discover the meaning of the faith all of us both live and struggle to live. Each of us does it differently because our experiences are different, but those varied experiences interact with each other, forming the fine interwoven network of Catholic life. However, this net, like any net, consists mostly of holes, so that when the net "catches" the experiences which are our history, our culture, much of it goes through the holes, because no human system can possibly express and embody every aspect of creation. But the net does hold a great deal, indeed it holds things we might, sometimes, prefer to throw back in the sea. Instead we need to look at the catch, understand it, sort it, but since this is a very unusual kind of net, what happens next is that what has been caught becomes, somehow, part of the fabric of the net itself, the new self-awareness of Catholicism. That is as near as I can get to expressing something of the process by which our ecclesial reality changes, as the people who compose it re-discover, through dynamic interchanges of ecclesial culture, the meaning of their existence as people of faith.

My Process of Re-Discovery

What are the things caught in the net that have motivated my own process of re-discovery? I don't apologize for taking the time to talk about this, because it seems to me that it is essential for all of us to understand how our experience shapes our ecclesial understanding, and to undertake our re-discovery *consciously*, not driven by experience but using it. This is something one may do, initially, just to preserve one's sanity and sense of self, yet the individual experience is not an isolated thing. Each person experiences things that are interwoven with the experience of others at many points, and which together form the whole cultural experience of a given time and place. In the case of people with a specific faith-identity, this experience—common and personal—is interpreted in terms of particular religious language—itself, again, the product of generations of reflection on experience. As a writer, it is my job to be aware of the growth and change of language which we call theology, and my own personal experience is my starting point in understanding how that works. The various categories of my experience are shared with many others, yet they are also mine—the net is made of little knots, meaningless alone, yet together forming something immensely strong and useful.

Age and European Background

In the categories of experience, first there is my age. I shall be sixty this year, and I became a Catholic in 1943 at the age of sixteen, in the middle of a world war. I was received into the Church and attended Mass in a church lit only by altar candles, because of the blackout, and I came to Mass one morning to find the church a mass of rubble. I had Jewish relatives who had escaped from Austria just before the frontiers closed, and we knew what might happen to us as a partly Jewish family if the Nazis crossed the narrow waters that inadequately protected England from invasion.

I was eighteen when the atom bomb was dropped, so the experience of war, yet with memories of a pre-war world, culminated in the ushering in of the "nuclear age," whose significance took time to become clear, and at the same time that "the bomb" ended the war, the facts of what was only later called the Holocaust began to be told.

My "spiritual life" as I learned (and later unlearned) to call it, was that of the time. I learned Catholic spirituality before Vatican II, was nurtured on Thomas à Kempis and Abbot Marmion and Janet Erskine Stuart and Pascal and Bernanos and all those people. At art school in wartime London, I sat on the grass in the park in my lunch hour and read Dame Julian, and historical novels about the persecution of Catholics under Elizabeth I. I swallowed it all, good and bad, with undiscriminating enthusiasm. Later, already married and with a growing family (growing in both senses) I encountered Thomas Merton, became somewhat intoxicated with him, and then, as it were, "grew up" with him, as he struggled, explored, and changed. I lived through the excitement and upheavals of Vatican II, the shock of Charles Davis's decision to leave the Church, and chaos of the liturgical changes. I was able to feel both the loss of loved customs and the hope of newness. So I have had time to add my own span of experience to my strong sense of history. I have read the strange stories of Christianity and learned to recognize that corruption, timidity, and sheer blindness in the government of the Church are not new, and exist alongside all that is passionate, divinely energetic and alive in the same tradition.

Secondly, therefore, there is my European background, out of which my sense of history grows, which has enabled me to make sense of much of the contemporary experience. I have dual citizenship, but I was born and raised in England and my outlook and nostalgias are English. So my sense of Catholicism is bound up with my awareness of roots in the ancient churches and shrines of England, which in turn have their roots in a long pre-Christian past, inheriting its symbols, its demons, and its mystical awareness. I know the importance of place, and roots, and I know the crucial but hard-to-define phenomenon of culture—the way a group of people feel, think, expect, react, and always assume that their way is the normal way, and that others are "foreign" and strange. I also know, more perhaps than most Americans do or have done until recently, that landscape is not just "nature." In England, landscape is the result of centuries of interaction between land and people, creating unique patterns, for good or ill. So, history and ecology, religion and culture, are linked and inseparable in my experience and in my theology.

Family and Community

Thirdly, there is the fact that I've raised a large family, and they grew up in the sixties and seventies, through all those times of the sexual revolution, the hippies and drop-outs and the rise of the drug culture. Now my children are raising families of their own, having survived all those things, but by no means unscarred. In their consciousness and also in mine is the awareness that the world looks different when you see it with eyes which have learned skills of seeing through the women's movement and the peace movement, and all of it under the constant shadow of possibily—even probably—nuclear annihilation. I learn from them, from their suffering and their dreams and their failures and their successes, their values and their desires. Through them I am in touch with a changed culture, different religious experiences and different ecclesial expectation—or lack of expectation.

One more strand in my experience—that of community, especially community for the sake of the marginalized. At one time I had the experience of rural community in Scotland, devoted to the needs of the mentally ill, and based in a farm. That chaotic but rewarding experience reinforced the sense of the land as the literal basis of human life and community, land as the source of wealth and health, land as God's gift, not as a commodity to be exploited for private gain. And more recently my experience of community has been in this country, involved in providing a place of hospitality for homeless women and children, and in finding ways to create low-cost housing. In my discovery of myself as a feminist, this experience of life with and for marginalized women has been radicalizing.

Making Sense of Experience

That's a lot of very varied experience. But for me it all comes together, and all of it has been part of my own re-discovery of Church. This has come about because, for sheer spiritual survival, I had to find a way to make sense of all this—and "making sense" of varied experience is precisely the motivation of all genuine theological discovery. Being a person who reads, I read—at each stage and turn of my life I asked questions and demanded answers. I have a naturally enquiring mind which asks "Why" about everything from the nutritional content of bread to papal authority. So in my need to re-discover ecclesial reality out of all this, I didn't only read theology (especially biblical studies), I read books on biology and the new physics, on world food production, on the history of women and the women's movement, on organizational culture, and lots more. I am not saying this in order to demonstrate my wide reading—it is sometimes so wide it might better be termed random—but because it seems to me very important to recognize that we live in a time when we have tools for understanding the human situation, and the human life within creation, in ways that have never been possible before. At the same time we as Catholics have experienced an opening of the Scriptures of an unprecedented kind, and the two kinds of knowledge—the apparently secular and the apparently sacred—come together, so we discover that this dualism is as false as all the other dualisms which opposed nature and grace, flesh and spirit.

A New Understanding

For me, as for many others, the experiences of the past decades have shattered many comforting and apparently coherent ways of thinking, and forced me to find new ways to understand and live. The Church I joined at sixteen—or rather my understanding of the Church I joined—was a coherent, intellectually satisfying system. It was a true guide and support and, more importantly for me, it was the context in which innumerable amazing people had flourished, their lives a promise that my own life could be different, more exciting, and stranger than those I saw around me. But the impact of the experiences I have sketched dismantled much of the coherence and comfort. I remember the shock I felt on the day I first realized how much of theology, how many doctrinal definitions (not to mention Canon Law) were simply designed to justify a power-system which had grown more entrenched and more self-convinced through the centuries. Once that shattering realization dawned I also began to realize how effective this system was in preserving allegiance by guilt-creating mechanisms and this awareness was reinforced by realizing that both the passion for power and the guilt-creating spirituality were denounced by Jesus, who saw them at work in his own religious tradition.

My experience of working with marginal people, especially women, made me aware of how the social system creates and maintains marginality for its own purposes, which it justifies in exalted terms, and how religion sets up the same mechanisms and re-inforces them with religious sanctions. But what is the alternative? Hierarchy is not a Catholic invention, it is something the Church picked up because that is how the world operates. But, however historically understandable and even effective it may be, for me it is no longer possible to say "church" and mean primarily any kind of hierarchical structure. Hierarchy is not of the essence, it is something the church developed because, collectively, it seemed the obvious thing to do, even though in so doing the plain message of Jesus about the danger of domination and misuse of power were ignored, or somehow "spiritualized." Even if the structure were entirely populated by saints and sages—and indeed it has contained a goodly population of both—the shape of it does not seem to me to reflect the pattern of creation. That is where my encounter with what modern biology and physics is telling us has helped us to re-discover what "church" can mean, and be.

An introduction to systems theory simply made it impossible to think of the living reality of Christian community in terms of dominance and control, however kind and well meant. The insights of biology and physics show us a universe in which each particle is part of a system, and is in itself a system, all interdependent and alive, none dominant yet each needing every other, from subatomic particles to the solar system, and beyond.

Model of the Saints

Scientists sometimes find themselves using the language of mysticism to describe what they discover. They dare to use the word "love" to describe that power in the observed universe which generates and regenerates, unconquerable, overcoming death, in a creation intricately ordered and yet allowing glimpses of the transcendence which both completes and confounds the order we can understand. So as one concept of church fell apart, another shone through—and it was confirmed both by my own experience and by the stories of those amazing characters, the saints and mystics, who to me had always been the real bearers of the stream of life which is Catholicism. Their hopes, dreams, and battles (often with the dominant ecclesial institutions), their sufferings and achievements, were the heart of the tradition. They (the known and unknown saints and heroines and heroes) were the creation of the true ecclesial culture which no amount of ecclesiastical timidity, prejudice and blindness could completely distort.

But the most important thing about the saints was that the church they lived and felt in their bones was that interdependent reality of God and humankind which is proclaimed in the gospels. In the saints, and those who gathered around them and shared their vision, the reign of God proclaimed by Jesus was re-discovered and lived, however briefly. For me and for many the re-discovery of Scripture was the thing that renewed the whole sense of what "church" is about, and made it possible not only to go on calling one's self a Christian but to re-discover the sense of truth and vitality in the whole Catholic experience, which has never wholly died, and renews itself in every age and place.

Re-Discovery of Scripture

Like many others, I re-discovered Scripture, especially through the experience of study with others. I'd like to give an example of the kind of thing I mean, from a group experience I've been involved in. One of the things that goes on at Wellspring House, where I live, is a training program for lay people who feel called to serve the poor in their own country. The two-year program begins with five weeks of intensive orientation, and the heart of that five weeks is the daily study of Mark's gospel, right through. But at the same time the trainees are doing social analysis, having first-hand experience of the effects of poverty locally, and learning the reasons for it. They see films and attend workshops and read books which open them up to the social and economic realities of our world, and daily they begin to put all this together with their reading of Mark's gospel. The effect of this is mind-blowing. Their old categories and assumptions are challenged, a new awareness of the reality of Jesus and his message breaks through. It is disturbing, it can seem to demolish what had appeared essential. But it is exciting, life-giving, it is a conversion experience, and it is lasting. And people do it together, supporting each other, agonizing, exploring, sometimes crying, sometimes laughing.

This is the kind of thing I mean when I talk about re-discovering church, and my own experience of community itself illumines the experience, and is illuminated by it. It is not only the encounter with the gospel in a new way, in the light of the modern experience and modern scholarship, but a re-discovery in the context of community, creating an experience of church which itself reflects the experience of those who met Jesus and discovered a different vision of reality. That was the experience of church to which Jesus introduced people and which he invited them to re-create in other places—a new kind of community based on awareness of the love of a non-patriarchal and passionately loving Father. It was a community which re-created relationships in the image of friends sharing food and life.

Let me try, in the short time I have, to indicate how, for me, the re-discovery of church in this sense is both nourished and illumined by my own past and present experience. I have suggested that the image of reality offered by systems theory helped me to understand a reality which grows from the grassroots, is de facto decentralized in thought, feeling and action and yet nourished by a common tradition and pursuing common goals.

I see this church alive and heroic among the persecuted people of Central and South America, in the slums of Chicago or the mountains of Appalachia where some of our mission trainees have worked, and in groups bursting out in middle-class parishes. But I also see this church, moved by the same spirit, in people gathered across boundaries of denominations, and even of faith and un-faith, as human beings responding to the irrepressible life of God within them, coming together to create new possibilities. The life that persists for years in a seed lying in the desert, only to spring into flower when rain falls, is the same spirit that can slowly and painfully begin to blossom in a human life that has from the beginning been so deprived of love and hope that it seemed to have shriveled to nothing. And just as the seed's possibility of blooming when the rain comes depends on the intricate network of life-support systems that surround it, ready to release nourishment, so a human person can only grow within a nurturing network of care and understanding and opportunity—a community, in some sense a church: that is, a gathering of people drawn by a hope and desire for new life, expressing that life in common symbols and common action.

But it is not enough that people come together to seek and create freedom, justice, true worship in little isolated groups. The nature of a church, as opposed to just any kind of community, is to be local, but also to be part of the life-giving network which actually makes it possible for people in the local gatherings to *be* church. The existence of a common language to express the reality which is both sought and lived is not the creation of any one group, or of its leaders, or any gathering of leaders. It is developed over time, and among many changes, in response to events. It varies from place to place because each place has its own memories, its own holy places, its own historical griefs and triumphs, but each can recognize the common symbols and energizing dreams. This is what we call tradition—it is difficult to define because it is a kind of essence of culture, expressing the reality of a whole historical experience in symbol and story and ritual. Tradition is carried within a whole people and in the local gatherings, it is compressed into definition, and the definition is later taken apart, mixed yet again with the historical experience, dissolved, changed and re-defined. And in each cycle it is in places where people are drawn together by the common vision, suffering, struggling, failing, enduring, and celebrating, that the tradition is formed, tested and reformed. It is a long history, and it can never be arrested and encapsulated, but only encountered in the ever-new living of the gospel experience.

Re-Discovering a Vision

I've re-discovered the church from the ground up, and it has been a stormy and painful experience. For years, as a mother, I tried to justify the church to my children; eventually they were among those who forced me to re-discover the church for myself. There have been times when I felt I had lost too much, that the historical glory, the sweet strength of the mystics, the depth of symbol and celebration, the recurring beauty of festivals, were draining away from me as I was obliged to recognize the existence of false, demeaning spirituality, of deception, power-seeking and cowardice as prevailing influences in the body I had joined with such enthusiasm as an adolescent. But I don't think I've lost those good things, I believe I have discovered anew how they do grow, fallibly but truly, from that unique explosion of divine energy which we call the Incarnation.

In many ways this is a painful time to be a Catholic. We seem to be in danger of losing a vision which had been regained after long struggle, and more and more people are being driven to conclude that the historical shape of authority in the church has more to do with the human desire for power and control, and the human ability to hide that motive under religious language, than with the gospel of human solidarity and the hope of the reign of God. But now, new ways of decision making, and organizing, the experience of the effectiveness of decentralized grass-roots movements, the experience gained through support groups (such as those of the women in our house), new understandings of how culture and community occur—many such things confirm with growing assurance the vision and practice of Jesus himself, and of those of his followers who, through the ages, have never lost hope that a different way was indeed possible, "on earth as it is in heaven." The tradition has never been lost, and it is strong and alive. The way the tradition is institutionalized can take many forms and has taken many.

One of the truly hopeful things about our time is that we no longer have to pick up uncritically whatever models of institution are around—Roman Empire, feudal monarchy, or corporate business. We are not doomed to discover by trial and error only that some models are essentially inappropriate to the gospel vision. We can understand the way groups and cultures grow and operate, we can perceive weaknesses and learn ways to correct them. There are no perfect models, but we can choose with more wisdom and learn with more humility, in touch with so many levels of created life, so many manifestations of the intricate beauty of God's work in which humankind has a central but not separate role to play.

The gospel vision of a community of interdependent people, living as brothers and sisters, is real and possible, and that is the heart of the experience which is church. It is possible—but we can refuse it or muddy it or destroy it. Sometimes it seems that the power of evil in the world is so great that nothing can stop it. But re-discovering the church means re-discovering hope, because in a world full of pain, fear and wickedness there are so many places where people come together to create and live the possibility of God's reign, in endurance and in joy. And this is really what the church is about.

A Pilgrim's Progress in a Catholic University

TIMOTHY O'MEARA

In early times in all cultures pilgrims went by foot to their spiritual destination. Many of the psalms in the Old Testament give witness to the pilgrims' journey to the Holy City of Jerusalem. In medieval times Chaucer framed his great masterpiece around a group of pilgrims journeying to the shrine of Thomas à Becket. In his famous allegory John Bunyan wrote of Christian, his hero, searching for the celestial city. In this poetic sense all of us are pilgrims journeying in search of our ultimate destiny.

Childhood Memories

My pilgrimage began sixty years ago tomorrow in Cape Town on the second story of the family bakery. My two brothers and I were fortunate to have been raised in a large family setting which included our grandmother and all sorts of cousins, uncles and aunts. My father was an Irishman, a businessman of integrity with a sense of humor and a great interest in people. My mother was of Italian descent, liberated without being combative, deeply spiritual with a slight air of the mystic. South Africa at the time was politically dominated

23

by certain kinds of condescending colonial English, and by Calvinist Afrikaners who referred to Catholics as *Die Roomse Gevaar*—The Roman Danger. We were a minority within a minority, but I certainly didn't look upon myself that way at the time. We lived in a mixed neighborhood. On the second floor of the bakery's garage there was a large hall which we rented out as a Black Christian Church. Our house was always full of people: Italians, Irish, Cape Coloureds, Xhosas, English, Afrikaners, Portuguese and Indians; Catholics, Protestants, Jews and Mohammedans; bakers, plumbers, bookkeepers, carpenters, police, doctors, servants, lawyers and priests. Everyone was welcome: many came—some to stay, a few to die. If the sons objected to the traffic, my mother would simply say, "Then I don't understand what is meant by being a Christian." In this rich environment, the family gave us a great stability and intrinsic belief in our Catholic faith.

My school day memories go back to the Loretto Convent and the Irish Christian Brothers. My theological training—if I might call it that—started with the penny catechism; then the sixpenny catechism; then the New Testament, almost to the point of knowing it by heart; followed by *Fortifying Youth,* a book published by the Irish Christian Brothers; and finally two massive volumes of Dr. Rumble's *Radio Replies.* I spent a good deal of my youth thinking about doctrinal and moral questions, often trying to analyze them in a mathematical sort of way. Instinctively I believed that all of theology was already known. Somebody, somewhere, really understood it all. Perhaps it was that awesome figure, Father Gavan Duffy, the Catholic chaplain at the University of Cape Town, and the only Jesuit I ever saw in South Africa.

I also had the instinctive belief that mathematics was known once and for all, probably discovered by Euclid or Pythagoras. I still have vivid memories of learning algebra and geometry from the Christian Brothers. I can still see in my mind's eye the page in my geometry book with the proof of Pythagoras' theorem. I had an insatiable appetite for solving mathematical problems even to the point of doing them for fun during my summer vacations. My parents were proud of my ability in mathematics—

and also a bit disappointed as they realized this interest would take me far from the family bakery.

Doctoral Studies

After graduating from the University of Cape Town, I left my homeland and started the second stage of my pilgrimage as a doctoral student at Princeton University. During my student days there I lived in the Graduate College, mixing with doctoral students from all disciplines and from all parts of the world. In retrospect I think that experience was as valuable, if not more valuable, than the mathematical training which I received at the university. At the same time, I cannot recall a single student or professor in mathematics at Princeton who was a Catholic. I did, however, seek out a very small group of Catholics from other disciplines who lived at the Graduate College with me. I also knew that prominent Catholic and distinguished mathematician, Marston Morse, who was not at the university but at the Institute for Advanced Study. During those days I met and married Jean, whose influence on me and my thinking has been profound. Her first and most decisive move was to give me a choice—between her and my constant companion in Southern Africa, Europe and America—my 1.0 litre Black Shadow motorcycle. To this very day I believe I made the right choice.

It was not until my second year as a doctoral student that I began to understand that mathematics was an ever expanding universe. My thesis advisor at Princeton was Emil Artin, one of the great algebraists of the century. Unfortunately, or perhaps fortunately, he offered me no advice in the selection of a thesis topic. I think it was a fluke that I got started at all. But once I did, a whole new world opened up to which I would devote an incredible amount of time and energy for over a quarter of a century. In the 1950s and 1960s and even the 1970s I had a view of mathematical truth which I might call absolutist, in the sense that I viewed mathematics as the only branch of knowledge in which you could be absolutely sure of what you were talking about. Not even Jean could knock that out of me. It was not until I became a provost that I realized that there were areas of life in which logical thinking could prove to be disastrous. Nevertheless I found that my mathematical way of analyzing, when properly used, was an invaluable tool in my job as provost.

Arriving at Notre Dame

After my graduate student days at Princeton, Jean and I went to the University of Otago in New Zealand for three years, then returned to Princeton for several years where I was both a faculty member at the university and a member of the Institute for Advanced Study. Finally, thanks to the persuasion of Marston Morse and Father Theodore Hesburgh, and the two mathematicians, Arnold Ross and Hans Zassenhaus, we came to Notre Dame in 1962. At last we were no longer in the minority!

My most productive days as a mathematician have been at Notre Dame and indeed I have kept my mathematics alive during my ten years as provost. I am not going to talk about my research except to say that it is in areas intersecting with modern algebra and the theory of numbers, and that the title of my new book with Alex Hahn is *The Classical Groups and K-Theory*. On the motivational side, however, I have been fascinated with the mysterious interplay between good mathematics and reality. Consider for example, the lines, triangles, squares and circles of Euclid. These are examples of forms that occur to us through our experience in nature. People— mathematicians—then study relationships among all sorts of these forms in increasing degrees of abstraction based only on the intrinsic harmony which is found in the relationships that unfold. Centuries later some of the relationships derived in total abstraction come back to earth and allow us to explain nature or even to change it. There is an intrinsic harmony then between mathematical forms, nature and the mind. That is what I find fascinating. That is what I find mysterious. Just take yourself back in time. Can you imagine the mathematics of the Babylonians, leading to the discovery of algebra by the Arabs in the Middle Ages, ultimately providing Newton with a framework for the calculus and his laws of gravitation which finally explained what held the heavens in their place? Who would have believed that mathematical logic, as abstract as abstract can be, would unlock the door to an instrument as revolutionary to our society as the computer? If these are not visible signs of the hand of God at work, then I would like to know what is.

Second Vatican Council

Our arrival at Notre Dame coincided with the Second Vatican Council. Little did I know at the time what impact the work of the Council would have on the growth and development of the church and the effect which it would ultimately have on our lives. In any event, I was a distant observer of the Second Vatican Council during the 1960s, occasionally wide-eyed at some of the developments, but always protected in my remote mathematical world. It was not until the 1970s that I began to appreciate the real questions that we as a Catholic people had to come to grips with—the role of the laity, the role of women in the Church, struggles for liberation in the Third World, questions of human sexuality. For the first time I realized what I had already realized twenty years earlier in the case of mathematics—that theology also was a process of growth and development. After all, how could the old theology of a just war have been applied to the nuclear age? Surely ethical questions had to be thought through anew in the light of advances in medical science. I attribute this growth of mine to various factors—an increased awareness in our society, in the Church, and especially at Notre Dame; vigorous discussions at the dinner table with our children who were now in their teens (we have four daughters and one son); and last but not least, the invaluable experience of serving as provost under Father Hesburgh, my greatest teacher, from whom I gained a sense of vision of the Church and of the university.

If I consider, on the basis of my experience as a scholar, as provost and as a Catholic, the most important areas for

growth and development among Catholic universities today,
I find two.

Catholics in Intellectual Life

First, I believe that it is essential that we take our place among
the great and influential universities of our country. From their
very inception, Catholic universities have been tied to the aspirations of American Catholics. During the last century and the
first half of this century, these have been the aspirations of an
immigrant people. Now as these aspirations are changing, we
must be responsive to new challenges for leadership at a higher
level of academe. We must become increasingly influential in
our society on the one hand and in the Church on the other,
through highly creative contributions to the arts and sciences,
technology, the professions and public service. We have a special
responsibility to encourage increased participation of Catholics
in the intellectual life. We still have to ask the rhetorical question
posed by John Tracy Ellis in the 1950s: "Where are the Catholic
intellectuals?" We must emphasize the fact that the quest for
knowledge is part of our search for God and therefore a natural
source for sanctifying our lives.

In today's secular society, it is at last possible for scientists
and people of faith to converse in a civilized way. Unfortunately
this is often accomplished by a sort of protocol which keeps
science and religion in separate compartments. This has certainly
been my own observation from my days as a graduate student
at Princeton to the present time. But at a Catholic university we
have a special challenge to make sure that the door between the
life of the mind and the life of the spirit is kept wide open. In
our tradition of faith seeking understanding, it is essential that
we be engaged in and wholeheartedly committed to the creative
process. We cannot simply be reactionary bystanders or critical
commentators. We must reverse a cultural condition in which
caution squelches intellectual curiosity. These are matters at the
very heart of our existence as Catholic academic communities.
Ideally, such growth needs not only the tolerance but the encouragement of the hierarchy. There will always be tensions between
democracy and authority, between teaching and research, and

between conserving and growing. It is how we resolve these tensions in our own universities that will determine whether we are reactive to society or progressive within it, and the extent to which our students and our ideas will influence American and Catholic culture in the 21st century.

Catholic Identity

Our second and more difficult problem, one that we will always have to grapple with, is how, in a pluralistic society such as ours, we can be ecumenical in spirit while maintaining a predominant and articulate Catholic presence on the faculty. Without that presence it will simply be a matter of time before our Catholic universities follow the rest of American higher education on the road to secularization. I have no doubt that the surest way to maintain our Catholic identity is through a partnership between our founding religious orders and the laity. In the early American church lay people were loyal contributors, passive and defensive, but not partners. Now, thanks in large measure to generations of missionaries and religious, we have a well-educated Catholic population. Following the Second Vatican Council, vocations to the priesthood and religious life have decreased sharply, while the role of the laity has changed from one of dependency to one of shared responsibility, a shared responsibility which embraces women as well as men, theologians as well as scientists, and, in a search for unity, members of other religions as well.

Shared Responsibility

The potential of this shared responsibility derives, obviously, from the sheer number and expertise of the laity, and, more importantly, from a straightforward independent American way of questioning things and looking at the world. But shared responsibility requires active involvement as well as shared consequences. Therefore all of us, religious or lay, men or women, people of all faiths, must focus not only on our teaching and research, but on sustaining and deepening the religious character of our university communities as well as providing for their evolution and continuation.

In conclusion, let me mention two things. First, how satisfying I have found the experience of preparing for this Marianist Award lecture. And second, how rewarding it is to speak with you about the vision which is shared by the University of Notre Dame and the University of Dayton and which is so important to the future of Catholic higher education. As we at Notre Dame continue our pilgrimage under the leadership of our new president, Father Edward Malloy, I find especially apt the words of T.S. Eliot:

> *We shall not cease from exploration*
> *And the end of all our exploring*
> *Will be to arrive where we started*
> *And know the place for the first time.*
>
> Little Gidding

Realizing Catholicism: Faith, Learning, and the Future

Walter J. Ong, S.J.

1

When he asked me to accept the great honor of the 1989 Marianist Award, the President of the University of Dayton, Bro. Raymond L. Fitz, S.M., suggested that in my response to the presentation of the award I might comment on the relationship of scholarship and the Catholic faith as this relationship has appeared to me in the course of my own scholarly and faith life. This is what I propose to do. I shall understand scholarship here in the broadest sense of learning as embracing both humanistic and scientific subjects. My brief remarks could not begin to be theoretically exhaustive but will be by way of personal reflection.

Perhaps more than on anything else, these reflections turn on the meaning of Catholicism and some ways in which this meaning has been realized in our times. "Catholic" is often interpreted as meaning "universal." In fact, it appears to mean much more. The early Latin-speaking branch of the church had at its disposal in its original Latin the term *universalis*, from which our "universal" derives. But in the so-called Nicene Creed we do not find, "Credo . . . in unam, sanctam, universalem, et apostolicam ecclesiam," that is, "I believe . . . in the one, holy, universal, and apostolic Church," but rather, "Credo in unam, sanctam, catholicam, et apostolicam ecclesiam," that is, "I believe in the one, holy, catholic, and apostolic Church." The Latin Church—so-called, we must remember, not because Latin was a special liturgical language, but because Latin was simply the language people in this part of the world had spoken in their ordinary life—refrained from using its own term *universalis,* preferring the Greek term *katholikos* instead. Why? Short of a massive historical study, perhaps a look at the etymologies of the words can offer a clue.

UNIVERSAL AND CATHOLIC

The terms "universal" and "catholic" approximate one another but are set up not quite the same way. *Universalis,* "universal," is formed out of the roots of *unum,* one, and *vertere,* to turn. Details of the etymology are not quite clear, but the image one gets is that of describing a circle by turning around one point. The circle includes everything within it. But it is a line, and the line seemingly excludes whatever falls outside it. It has an inside and an outside. *Katholikos,* "catholic," works differently. It means throughout-the-whole: it combines *kata,* which has among its meanings through or throughout, and *holos,* which means whole and indeed comes from the same proto-Indo-European root as our own English word "whole."

Note that "throughout-the-whole," *katholikos,* "catholic," does not suggest a boundary as "universal" does. It is expansive, open, growing. If the whole gets larger, what is "throughout the whole" gets larger too. This concept "throughout-the-whole" recalls Jesus' description of the kingdom of God as leaven, yeast, placed in dough. In Matthew 13.33 (echoed in Luke 13.21) we read, "The reign of God is like yeast which a woman took and kneaded into three measures of flour. Eventually the whole mass of dough began to rise." Yeast is a plant, a fungus, and it grows. It has no limits itself, but is limited only by the limits of whatever it grows in. The Church, understood as Catholic in this way, is a limitless, growing reality. Growth marks the Church often spectacularly in our own day. By contrast with the Church of a century ago, the present Roman Catholic Church shows itself as more and more conspicuously Catholic, representing all the races and regions of humankind. The faces of the participants in the Second Vatican Council and the appearance of its Catholics from across the world in the media today make it quite evident that the Roman Catholic Church is no longer a simply Western or European phenomenon.

This sense of Catholicism as a living and growing reality I believe has been a dominant feature of my own sense of the relationship between scholarship and faith. Earlier, I perhaps did not formulate the idea to myself or others so explicitly, but I know it was there, working away in my subconscious or unconscious.

2

The age in which I grew up was an intellectually exciting time. Many frontiers ultimately affecting the relationship of scholarship and faith were opening up at once. Some of these frontiers overlapped, and they can be discussed in various ways. Here I should like to view them insofar as they were the heritage of the Romantic Movement, which reference books tell us took place throughout Europe between 1770 and 1848 and which was most marked initially in northern Europe. In fact, of course few movements can be confined to the neat datings which reference works assign them. Belatedly, long after 1848, in the early and mid-twentieth century, the Romantic Movement had a tremendous, and I believe hitherto little discussed, effect in the Roman Catholic Church.

The Romantic Movement was, among other things, a reaction to the extreme rationalism of the preceding age of the Enlightenment. The two contrasting movements are not easy to describe in their entirety, but for our purposes here we can note that, whereas the Enlightenment undertook to reduce everything to rational explanation, Romanticism was not so sure that such reduction was entirely possible. By contrast with the Enlightenment, the Romantic Movement was more interested in the dark, obscure side of existence, in nature as a growing and largely uncontrollable actuality, interested in the limitless, the expansive, less interested in fixity and more interested in development. Romanticism preferred the countryside to the city. It tended to dwell on what was not fully formalized, what had not been brought fully under rational human control (this does not mean necessarily the irrational, for reason does not and never can completely control everything: reason is always surrounded by a context beyond its control). Romanticism was preoccupied often with the dark, the obscure, favoring the boundless imagination over neater, abstract thought.

Quite evidently, Romanticism was not invented in 1770. Some Romantic preoccupations are as old as the human race. For example, we find preoccupations of a Romantic sort in the Bible, perhaps most notably in Job, we find them in Virgil, in Shakespeare and in much Renaissance humanism, and in many other places and times, both in the West and elsewhere in the world. But, although traces of Romanticism have in such fashion always been around, never anywhere until the later 1700s was there a large Romantic *Movement*, a widespread, generalized surge of interest in a view of existence setting itself self-consciously against reliance on clear-cut, rationalist formulations. In the book *Rhetoric, Romance, and Technology* I have suggested that the outburst we now know as the Romantic Movement was made feasible by the build-up of knowledge over the centuries, especially since the invention of print in Europe in the mid-1500s. By the 1700s there was a store of knowledge on hand, much of it in our modern, superrational scientific form, immeasurably greater than ever before, so that human beings generally—and not just a few—could without too much fear dwell and dwell on the dark side of existence, which had been there all along. At one's back, as one faced into the darkness, stood rationalized knowledge at hand, immeasurably greater than what was available before the accumulation made possible by print. In the world of thought, the store of stabilized knowledge counterbalanced a great deal of risk.

The Romantic Movement was sweeping and its effects are certainly permanent. I remember the remark of a colleague of mine at Saint Louis University a few years ago: "Books often contrast Romanticism with the Neo-Classicism that went before it. But Romanticism contrasts not only with Neo-Classicism. It contrasts with everything that went before it. Nothing like this had ever happened before, and it would affect the human mind and lifeworld permanently. Even anti-romantic movements from now all will be romantically cast." I believe this is true of anti-romantic movements in our world today. Looked on as a whole, even our science is romantic, too. However, science enlarges the field of rationality, as it does justifiably and necessarily, science itself is intimately aware today that the boundaries of science are not fixed in rationality but run off into darkness and into mystery.

THE CHURCH AND ROMANTICISM

In the earlier part of the twentieth century, one of the things that made Catholic intellectual life in my time especially interesting was that it was finally, belatedly, experiencing the fuller effects of the Romantic Movement, as we have described the movement here. The Church in its origins had been Mediterranean and curiously urban. In the early days of the Church, non-Christians tended to be considered, rather typically, countrified. We can see this in the word "pagan." The word "pagan" comes from the Latin word *paganus*, which means simply country person, country bumpkin—the same root that gives us the English word "peasant" and its cognates in many other European languages. In the West, the Church's intellectual heritage had been largely Greek, in the highly urban Platonic-Aristotelian tradition. Romanticism, as just noted, had developed largely in northern Europe, filtering southward slowly, and it tended to focus attention as never before on the country, the untamed, not on the city. The Christian faith of course had long been acclimated to the country, but its intellectual heritage had been largely of urban provenience. Romanticism provided new ways of focusing intellectually on the nonurban, the nondomesticated, the more purely natural.

Looking at Romanticism as concerned with the dark, the obscure, the rationally recalcitrant features of existence, the developmental, the natural, rather than the completely "formed," I have to note how much in the early twentieth-century intellectual world in which I grew up was marked by attention to such features. This was the age when, as instanced for example in the work of Freud, awareness was spreading of the force of the subconscious and unconscious in art, literature, history, politics, and the work of reason itself. It was the age when organic evolution was commanding more and more widespread attention and when ideas of evolution were spreading from the organic world to the study of all existence. Einsteinian physics had opened the way to a developmental cosmology, as against the older, fixed Newtonianism. Historicism—implemented by the massive documentation made possible by print—was taking over in all the humanities: in language studies, in literary studies, in political science, in philosophy, in biblical studies, and in theology.

In Catholic intellectual circles, the "Thomism," so-called, earlier taken for granted as a fixed, infrangible plenum was examined historically, and found to be in depth not really the basic teaching of St. Thomas Aquinas but an adaptation thrown together by later ages for reasons which were historically and culturally complex and not at all entirely conscious. Etienne Gilson's persuasion that Thomas was in a valid sense an "existentialist" drastically resituated Thomas and set on edge the teeth of those who had innocently believed themselves true programmatic Thomists. In biblical studies, Leo XIII's encyclical *Providentissimus Deus* in 1893 showed a certain hostility toward the historicism of non-Catholic scholars but was not entirely set against all historical exegetical studies, and, while the Modernist crisis, and much else that was developmental-historical at base, held back for some years the development of Catholic biblical studies and other historically grounded studies among Catholics, in 1943 the encyclical *Divino Afflante Spiritu* of Pius XII appeared, the Magna Charta of modern Catholic biblical scholarship. With it, the way to fuller study of the development of the Bible was open to Catholic scholars.

OUR FRONTIER MENTALITY

Of course, our own American self-consciousness, has taken much of its own distinctive shape in the world dominated by the developmental-historical interests we have been noting here. Ours is a frontier mentality, very likely more so than the mentality of any other country ever. We think of ourselves as frontier people, a people permanently and deeply involved in change. This self-image shows in our literature, our movies, our heroes, our heroines, our folklore of every sort. The frontier mentality has not always been well managed, for at the hands of those of us who are of European descent it has at times made for the oppression of those of us who are Native Americans and, less directly but just as really, for the oppression of those of us who are black. But the frontier mentality is not strange to any of us, those of more or less direct European descent, Native American, blacks, Hispanics, or more recent immigrants from across the world. It is a major part of us all, one way or another, and it suggests that the mind-set which I have here connected with Romanticism has a particular urgency on the American scene. In my own case, I feel confident that an at-homeness with the developmental-historical patterns we have been discussing here was strengthened by the United States milieu into which I was born. In this way, I believe that the scholarship-faith relationships in my own life were helped by the United States milieu.

For many, of course, the romantic concern with the dark, the obscure, the unfinished and developmental as against the bright, the totally clear, the fixed, appeared as a threat. Too much attention to history rather than to fixity, it was feared, would end in pure relativism, where questions of truth or falsehood were meaningless. It seemed to many that if knowledge could not be somehow lifted out of history and constituted in a landscape of timeless, discrete building blocks, nothing could be known and complete chaos would reign. But historicism, in depth, did not volatilize all knowledge. Far from that, it made knowledge more weighty. What appeared clear-cut could be true and could be understood, but it could not be understood merely in itself: it always connected with a great many other things. The situation was one not of destructive relativism but of constructive relationism. Truth can indeed be laid hold of, but truths are all related to each other and, when we know a given truth, we find it involved with other truths, all of which we cannot surface here and now.

3

The scholarship-faith question is affected today by the incommensurability of the universe as we know it today and the universe as persons in biblical times conceived of it. Although in a sense the relationship of Christianity to the future is always the same—Christianity is an incurably future-oriented religion—in another sense the relationship of Christianity to the future has changed almost beyond conceiving. Scholarship takes place in and devotes itself to a world of physical and psychological size and complexity totally unimaginable not only in biblical times but even a few hundred years ago, and we know that we are headed through ages of unknown duration to still greater unknown complexities. The human world that existed in the time of Christ was a world which had not the slightest idea that it was shaped to produce eventually spacecraft and computers or that such developments can be only beginnings of still newer creations of humankind. This world that recent discoveries have revealed, not the world as imagined by our predecessors, is the world in which Jesus was born and died. The eschatological future cannot be independent of this real created world. The interrelation of the two is not clear, but the relationship is undeniable and it raises stupendous theological questions involving modern science and modern humanities—questions to which, it appears to me, we do not even yet sufficiently attend, although I must admit the questions are so stupendous that I do not know how to go about compassing them. And the questions are stupendous even without the awful question of human suffering, some of which is due to the forces of nature but much of which is due to human villainy, and all of which we routinely advertise on our television screens so as to make disaster a permanent part of the human lifeworld as it has never been before.

THE CHALLENGE OF TECHNOLOGY

The world that God created understandably troubles us today. It troubles many persons largely because of its burgeoning technology, so far away, it seems, from the distinctively human, from nature. Some are inclined to blame our present woes on technology. Yet there are paradoxes here. Technology is artificial, but for a human being there is nothing more natural than to be artificial.

Technology can dehumanize us and at times has dehumanized us. But it can also humanize us. Indeed, technology is absolutely indispensable for many of our absolutely central humanizing achievements. Technology is needed for any scholarship. Writing is a technology, requiring artificial codes and complex equipment; as some of you are aware many of my own books and articles undertake to explain this at length. Writing does not simply reproduce oral discourse in visual (and tactile) form. it transforms thought, making possible thought patterns and making accessible kinds of material quite unavailable to a purely oral culture. Without the technology of writing, the kind of thinking that goes into the discourse we commonly use today is quite impossible—even the thinking that goes into much of our oral discourse, which is shaped by the thought patterns we know through writing and reading. Without writing, the kind of listening you have been engaging in here would have been impossible—even if you are bored.

Perhaps even more evidently than through writing, technology humanizes us through music. We speak of musical "instruments." Instruments are tools. The modern orchestra, made up of hundreds of astonishingly complex musical tools and machines—the organ must be described as a machine—is a triumph of high technology. Ancient Greeks and Romans could make music on "pipes of oaten straw" or perhaps on recorders (not the electronic kind of recorder, but the kind of recorder you blow into). You could play this simple kind of recorder by stopping the holes with your bare fingers. But the ancients were totally incapable of making any precision instrument such as the clarinet, much less a piano or an organ. Precision technology of any sort until just a few centuries ago terminated in something at about the level of a good pair of scissors. The modern orchestra is the result of technological developments of only the past three hundred years. Before that, all the deeply humanizing effects produced by the highly technological musical instruments in our orchestras were denied to human beings. Like all human developments, technology has its dangers, but it has its deep and mysterious humanizing effects, too.

4

What is the task of Catholic scholarship in the world we have described here? If the scholarship is truly Catholic, it will seek to understand the whole of actuality. It will keep itself moving on a quest which is impossible to realize entirely but which is promising always, and often exhilarating, even in the face of overwhelming human suffering and evil. For much evil, there is no human answer at all, but for the Christian, if there is not a simple answer, there is a response, in God's own response. The response is that we must counter evil with good. In the incarnation of the Son, in Jesus Christ, the infinite God responds to evil by entering into the human condition, with its suffering and its subjection to evil, to overcome suffering and evil by good, culminating in the obedience that Jesus expressed on the cross. We have a faith that seeks understanding—*fides quaerens intellectum*, as St. Anselm, in his learned humility, put it some 900 years ago. Our quest for understanding lives in Christian hope, a hope in Jesus Christ, who became incarnate in this world still opening more and more to our view. Since all this world is God's creation, all learning not only about God but also directly about this world can further our quest to understand our faith.

In my own life, the biblical and Catholic conviction that, however vast the universe in time and space, God made it all, has, I trust, been the sustaining force uniting faith and science and scholarship of all the kinds with which I have been in contact. The intellectual developments here discussed in relation to the romantic outlook have opened us to immeasurable cosmic vastness but should lead to no ungovernable fears. In my own life as in the lives of many others, St. Ignatius of Loyola's quiet insistence in his *Spiritual Exercises* that human beings are "created to praise, reverence, and serve God, our Lord," and thus to save their souls and that "The other things on the face of the earth are created" to help human beings in attaining this end, builds on this Catholic and biblical belief. Ignatius and his contemporaries of course had no idea of the magnitude of creation as we know it today. Ignatius' "on the face of the earth" has to be extended beyond measure today since our forays into space, far more extensive than Ignatius could ever have imagined. But if Ignatius could not help being limited in his vision, he nevertheless meant to be inclusive. Ignatius believed that God made all that existed outside God himself, even though he had very deficient paradigms for imagining what "all" was. Ignatius' faith and the depth of prayer response to that faith in the *Spiritual Exercises* were not measured by the deficient cosmic vision of his day. Nor was the faith and the depth of prayer of Guillaume Joseph Chaminade, when in 1817 he founded the Society of Mary, measured by the improved but, by present standards, still deficient cosmic vision of his time. Nor was the faith and the depth of prayer of Adèle de Trenquelléon, who with Chaminade founded the Daughters of Mary Immaculate in 1816. Christian faith and prayer go beyond such matters. Today, with our knowledge that we live in an evolving world, faith and prayer are faced into the future in new and breath-taking ways that merit our attention, but ways not discontinuous with the past.

TRADITION AND THE FUTURE

The Catholic Church builds on the past, of course, on tradition. But the faith is not retroactive. As I have earlier suggested, there is no way to recover the past, even if we wanted to. And who would want to? I have never met anyone who knows in scholarly detail any age of the past who would prefer that age to the present, however threatening and dangerous and ugly many things in the present may be. If you know the past in detail, it was in its own ways threatening and dangerous and ugly as well as beautiful and consoling. Tradition builds on the past but it always faces not into the past but into the future.

In the past and the present and the future, there is one constant that I can only point to here in closing, but that is supremely important. This is the individual, the "I" that each one of us is. Some four billion persons in the world today can say "I" or its equivalent in languages other than English, and every one of them means something completely different by the term. Yet only such beings can and must realize themselves in the love of others and in community. And only in such unique persons can either faith or scholarship exist. In this vast universe, spread through space and time, each of us relates to God in his or her own inimitable, personal way. This awareness gives us heart in faith and in scholarship both. It means that the ultimate values even of the exterior universe rest in the personal. For only persons can know and love.

In my end is my beginning. May I remind you now, as when I opened this talk, that there are innumerable other things to say about the relationship of faith and learning besides the few limited reflections I have advanced here. There are no bounds to the study of faith and to the realization of the potential of scholarship in God's created world. The object of our scholarship, humanistic and scientific, will continue to expand indefinitely for us.

The person of faith has no reason to fear that scholarship will expose anything incompatible with faith. This has been the assumption with which I have always lived, as other Christian scholars commonly have. The faith does not confront the universe. The faith penetrates the universe. However overwhelmingly huge and complex that universe may be, this is the universe in which the humanity of Jesus Christ is rooted, the universe in which the Son of God became a human being who died for us and rose to bring us to a new life. Our scholarship, like all else in our lives, rests on trust in the living and loving God.

Counsel, Commitment, Comfort and Joy

Sidney Callahan

My journey within Catholicism has been long and eventful, and always satisfying in the extreme. I had the good fortune to discover the pre-Vatican II Church in my late adolescence as I was struggling to grow up and find an intellectual ideal. Soon after my conversion I also began discovering love, marriage, childbirth, childrearing and domestic life with a great deal of manual labor and very little money. The Church validated these combined ideals of heart and mind, love and truth, family and scholarship—and helped me to pursue them.

Happily, I was not inhibited by the need to overcome childish resentments of Catholic schooling (I have never had a day of formal Catholic education), or the oppressive hand of misused authority. All my oppressive authorities and orthodoxies involved the secular assurances of anti-religious dogmatism. In my circles there reigned a great deal of Wasp worldliness along with Ivy League certainties adhered to by all right thinking people of the right sort. Becoming a Catholic at Bryn Mawr College in 1954 was definitely not the fashionable thing to do; my lapsed Calvinist southern military family was appalled, my professors were saddened to see one more good mind going to waste by embracing love, marriage, babies and Roman superstition.

I, for my part, was in ecstasy as a new Catholic and could not believe my good fortune in having been blessed with such a variety of riches. This classic "honeymoon" phase of my religious conversion has made me more tolerant that some of the sentimental pietism in certain Catholic devotions, the extremes of sweetness and light, can be a true reflection of the experience of certain temperaments at certain times of life. In my case this fervor probably had little to do with holiness and a lot more to do with youth, good health and erotic energy. However, even now in middle age, while the honeymoon may be over, the marriage is fruitful and happy and the well is still producing living water for me. I welcome this chance to share my experiences of faith; I can express my gratitude for the gifts of Counsel, Commitment, Comfort and Joy.

Counsel

I think of counsel as good counsel, or as a synonym for the wisdom of the Catholic heritage. The intellectual life and vocation became validated for me as I educated myself in Catholicism. I literally threw myself into mastering the Catholic religious heritage and benefited from the works of scholarship which were available in English. As I studied I felt confirmed in taking as my vocation or calling, the intellectual life of a Christian humanist. Catholic Christianity affirmed many beliefs about truth and reality which made it seem worthwhile to continually seek an intellectual life.

The idea that Truth *is*, and exists beyond and independently of the individual mind's construction is a great impetus for those who would seek truth. The idea of truth is one of the great ideas of the western world; we owe much of our civilization and science to the conviction that there is a rational reality which exists independent of human minds but is still accessible to human thinking. Our reason is vindicated by the belief in a truth toward which human beings are drawn.

Truth for Catholic believers, is also identified as the "I am" of God. When truth is identified with a divinity who is love, then truth and love are one. Truth and the intellectual quest need not be alien or austere; it can never be impersonal, sterile or value free. Once truth is seen as the personal, loving reality which divinely permeates all of creation, then the unity of the fabric of creation is assured. Everything to do with the intellectual effort to understand is worthwhile, "Whether you eat or drink, Whatsoever you do, Do it all for the love of Christ." Study and intellectual effort has intrinsic value for itself alone. This conviction that learning was good in itself and did not have to have a bottom line or practical use, kept me studying for long years at home before I could ever dream of going back to graduate school, or writing anything on my own.

I never felt that studying was an escape from life or beside the point. Once truth is seen as the underlying unity of creation, then study and pursuit of learning is getting at the center of things. All rivers will lead to the sea; the intellectual quest will uncover connections and structures which will be related. The more you know, the easier it is to learn, and the more you know there is to be learned.

This realization translated into time in the library means that a student has contemplative moments of great joy; there are flashes of intellectual ecstasy when you see that different bodies of knowledge are coming together, or you finally master a difficulty, and then say yes, "aha" I see it, I get it. The human mind comprehending, understanding and appreciating that one now knows is very much related to the core mysteries of reality and human consciousness. The student's work and effort to keep attention focused, to keep grasping with a challenge, falls away before the happiness of learning, knowing and understanding. The intellectual life has an intrinsic romance while it also requires detailed, disciplined work.

The intellectual life of study is a way to God through the wonders of the mind and the world. And God is infinite and truth is infinite. When I was a little girl I felt distress because I was sure that everything would already be known by the time I grew up, and there wouldn't be anything left for me to learn. I needn't have worried. God is a God of surprises with infinite variety and excitement to offer those who take the smallest step toward the Divine invitations. God is never, ever, boring.

The search for Truth, intrinsically wonderful, also turns out to be liberating and freeing. How many shackles and stereotypes have been left in the dust through inquiry, study and learning! To be educated is to be free. Good thinking and efforts to be reasonable and rational in all of one's personal thinking give one access to various critiques of current conditions. Mystifications and authoritarian oppressions of government, church, academia, medicine or economics—of the emperor's new clothes variety—come crashing down with sustained attention and thinking. On a more humble note, a person convinced of the effectiveness of rational thinking and effort can learn to do anything, including tax forms, motorcycle maintenance, statistics, computer programs, and how to follow inscrutable directions to put toys together on Christmas Eve.

The kind of disciplined thinking and effort which serves to see reality clearly can be turned inward upon the self, one's own personality and store of immaturity and craziness the flesh is heir to. Good thinking helps you grow up and become mature. New movements of cognitive therapy and reality therapy employ counseling techniques which point out and challenge erroneous irrational thinking patterns, which lead to personal disasters. "Why do you assume that you are entitled to a perfect life?" "Why do you think you must be perfect at all times?" "The dire effects or consequences you predict from event A are disproportionately exaggerated." And so on. Slowly the irrational can give way to reasoned wisdom in one's inner life. A lifelong dedication to truth and good counsel can forge the personal virtue of prudence, or "doing the right thing in the best possible way."

The dedication to reason turns out to be incredibly practical because rational truth is at the core of ultimate reality. Believers in divine truth are confident that conflicts and problems between different disciplines and ways to truth will be resolved in the long run. I am a firm believer that our Catholic heritage is founded upon the double foundation of reason and revelation. I do not believe because it is absurd, but because it is rational to do so. Faith goes beyond the certainty of evidence, but not counter to rational thinking.

This assertion of the essential unity of truth is far easier to make now than in the nineteenth century when religion and science seemed bent upon a collision course. Today it is possible to see science and philosophy and morality and theology as similar rational pursuits, trying to approximate and penetrate the truth of reality ever more completely. We now have assimilated ideas of the historical evolution of ideas and the existence of progressive changes in successive paradigms and worldviews. While no formulation can be all encompassing and complete, progress can be made and rationally tested against our experiences. Being a part of the progressive effort to intellectually understand reality is one of the most satisfying ways to live and work.

I have gradually seen what my own role as an intellectual should be. Happily, the vocation of thinking and scholarship is honored in Catholic life by our traditional respect for the great doctors of the Church, both male and female. One can also take heart by remembering the legion of unknown servants of the written word who copied and illuminated manuscripts, and thereby preserved traditions of learning in turbulent times. Today, we may get insight about our intellectual vocation rather slowly, but the film finally develops and the picture becomes clear. I find that as a psychologist I am drawn to study human self-consciousness, and our moral convictions and commitments. This is a domain of psychology where religion and moral philosophy overlap. How do we make moral decisions, and how does our personality affect our deliberations? At times I will address a more specific topic, such as reproductive decisions, but underlying this concern is the deeper interest in understanding how human beings are self-interpreting moral decisionmakers.

It takes courage in today's academia to undertake interdisciplinary work. We have all been professionally trained in narrow specialized competencies, and the academic reward structure reinforces specialization. One great liberating moment in my own interdisciplinary journey came when I could finally symbolically kill off my graduate school mentor in my academic superego. He had taught me that psychology was first of all a science, and operationalized empirical research counts as the most valuable enterprise. Now I know one must be daring and work on the most relevant problem, rather than go the narrow route which one's discipline or past training prescribes.

In my intellectual work and professional activities I try to put all my convictions and beliefs into practice. I attempt to teach undergraduates in a holistic interdisciplinary way, introducing students to the field of psychology and the importance of rational thinking and personal insight. I am less successful in trying to convey the idea of intellectual ecstasy and the romance of learning! Unfortunately, the discipline and detailed effort is less foreign to their idea of education as a boring, rite of passage. Naturally I struggle to try and improve my teaching semester after semester; oh, to be able to galvanize and excite as well as be a good coach.

I pray for energy and wisdom so that I will never burn out and be false to my intellectual vocation. I want to be of use and serve well. I pray before classes, and before talks that I may do as well as I can, and reach those who can make use of what I offer. I pray for guidance in choosing my writing projects. When something needs to be addressed, and I can do it, I try to overcome inertia and laziness. My prayer for wisdom becomes most fervent when I must take a controversial stand on some disputed point, such as abortion or surrogate motherhood. I fear being wrong and leading others astray, and on the other hand, I fear succumbing to the pressures of the dominant secular majority who make it difficult to take an unpopular point of view. I think the intellectual life requires an interesting mix of stoutheartedness and steadfastness, which must be complemented by flexibility and openness to rational inquiry and change. Obtaining and keeping up this paradoxical stance takes energy and commitment.

Commitment

No one comes to middle age without a new respect for the virtue of perseverance. How hard it is to keep on keeping on; to muster the energy to fight off inertia. In our affluent times it is easy to sink into our comforts and give up the struggle. The drive to make extra effort becomes more difficult as the hungry ego of youth becomes less insatiable.

There comes a point at which personal ambition no longer drives the work on, and one must work for internal, intrinsic reasons. This transition to inner directives, I find, entails finding a source of energy beyond the self. I must be able to receive grace in order to desire to desire. I most fear no longer caring about the truth or the good. Zest and enthusiasm tend to pale unless God gives inspiration to the effort. Novelty and the lust for excitement have long since been exhausted as a motive.

Here I think the experience of sacramental worship in community energizes and gives us commitment. Week after week we attend and worship and pray to receive spiritual food and be transformed. God hears us and answers our prayers for rescue and healing. Save us from atrophy, apathy and withering away. Keep us juicy. Refresh us, enspirit us, enliven us, and move us to take risks. We have to have a vision to keep growing and God does not fail to give us new dreams if we pay attention. Ask and you shall receive.

Catholics have rightly understood and been prepared for the fact that life will be hard. In the Church the cross has never been forgotten or ignored as a reality of Christian life. Our struggles only take new forms in our middle-class American soap operas. Life is always harder than you can ever imagine, but the resources given to meet the setbacks also are more abundant than one might conceive beforehand.

Frequent worship and prayer make the home truths more and more apparent. Experience teaches us with its lived authority. We become convinced that we must always "do what you are doing." We begin to understand the sacrament of the present moment and the fact that we are called to live fully moment by moment, right now. This simplifying truth gives us a depth of commitment, for we cannot put off anything into the future or be nostalgic for the past.

I have always been attracted to the little way of St. Therese, filtered through the writing of my mentor in faith, the great Dorothy Day. Dorothy is so American, so full of commonsense and holiness. Little by little, minute by minute, we live our way into the future and slowly become transformed and accomplish whatever we have been given to do. Books are written a page at a time; marriages are created daily, and children grow and careers are made, one day at a time.

Christians have to be prepared to do whatever it is important to do. One of the ways one decides what is important is to find out what is uniquely your own particular task to do. Living in time we have to make constant decisions about the best deployment of our forces. Sometimes this means that we will be doing great things in the world, and sometimes our task will be the most personal and private errand. We should be ready to either one, and not shrink from the call of public life or the call of the sick room.

God seems to surprise us here too. The invitations keep coming through when we pay attention. We are not ever sure where we are going but we seem to be going somewhere. Last month we had reports in the press of a new continent of galaxies discovered in the distant sky, so huge that no one ever thought to look for it. Our galaxy along with others in the universe seems to be hurtling toward this mysterious mass at enormous speed. This amazing new discovery has been named "the great attractor." I find this an apt metaphor for God's effect upon us; we recognize that we too are caught up in the energy field of The Great Attractor. This realization gives us a sense of movement and excitement, but also produces comfort and joy.

Comfort and Joy

My faith has been a great comfort to me, and along with all the other little old ladies, I am glad of it. I know the faith is supposed to afflict the comfortable as well; but we should not be afraid of admitting to great bouts of comfort and joy. Many have observed that in faith we move from a childlike faith, through rational critiques and intellectual understandings, and then come finally to "a second naivete." The final childlikeness is a "gift to be simple," as the Shakers would say.

In the more mystical experiential stage we feel that God cares for us as a mother, and is intimately a part of our lives. No matter is too small to bring up between friends. This assurance of God's care and presence within, produces an enormous sense of trust and comfort in times of trouble. My own sense of this maternal presence has accompanied an increase in Marian devotion, perhaps as a symbolic expression of this understanding of divine nurturing. Somehow when I say the great Marian prayers, I feel one with countless others over the centuries who have sought help—and received aid.

After all, even the most fortunate life will be filled with heartbreak, disillusionment, illness, betrayals of various kinds. If one loves others, you give up forever the stoic *apatheia* which can give emotional control through detachment and isolating distance. You will suffer disappointments from others and with your own inadequacies. The inability to help those one loves is a particular torture.

God comforts us in our suffering in many ways. First we know that the suffering is shared and we are never alone. God knows, even if the world and others are giving false testimony or dismissing the troubling concern. In God's eyes we can feel vindicated, and know that ultimate reality can only give ultimate victory to the truth. The psalms are wonderful devotions when one is being beset by persecution or worldly troubles.

The other great comfort is to know that suffering will not be useless and meaningless in God's purposes and plans. Our suffering can be used somehow in the divine economy and will not be in vain. Finally, death will be overcome and all our losses and sadness will be restored in the Kingdom. This hope and faith comforts us, although it does not seem to lessen the pain of loss in the short run.

I began to meditate the other day on what it would mean to truly "take away the sins of the world." Human beings would have to be made whole enough and liberated enough to act without weakness or inner divisions. And then these free whole persons would have to want to be good and do God's will. God would have to heal us and restore us and then inflame us with a desire for God and the kingdom. But of course, this is our faith, that somehow the kingdom will come and we will be transformed and live with God.

Comfort gives way to joy, so comfort and joy have always gone together. The Church tries in the liturgy to give depressed, glum Americans some glimmering of celebration and happiness. We have to learn to be happy, for we are basically afraid of joy most of the time and cling to the sureties of the land of gloom. It is hard to believe that the good news is real; that we are made to be joyful. Most holy people strike us as joyful and deeply happy, but it doesn't look easy to emulate.

I think we must learn to trust our joyful moments, those peak experiences of euphoria, which burst upon us from time to time. Those moments make us believe that the story is going to have a happy ending, and we will live to see it and dance at the marriage feast. Those moments of acute joy are precious and must be remembered and savored. They help us love more deeply and better still, trust our loving impulses. They inspire gratitude to God for consciousness and the graciousness of life.

Indeed, in looking back upon my journey in the faith my dominant response is gratitude. How deeply blessed we are to be alive, to know God, and be able to love and work. For me the Church has acted as it is meant to do, it has provided a sacramental encounter with Christ and the Holy Spirit. Our Catholic communion has given me counsel, commitment, comfort and joy. Grace has truly abounded.

What It Means to Be a Catholic in the United States in the Year 1991

John T. Noonan, Jr.

Deeply honored as I am by this award and deeply grateful for your generosity, I propose to offer in return a kind of declaration of faith. It is not an official creed. I do not pretend to be completely comprehensive. I do want to set out what the reading of history, literature, law, philosophy and theology and the lived experience of 64 years as a Catholic suggests to me as to what being a Catholic means.

Thirty years ago this year preparations were afoot for what was to be the most significant event in the history of the Catholic Church since the sixteenth century and one of the most significant religious assemblies ever convoked: the Second Vatican Council. For me, as for many observers, it also had a personal significance.

The Second Vatican Council

We came to Rome—we who had never seen a Council—holding to the belief that a General Council of the Church, acting in conjunction with the Pope, could, under the guidance of the Holy Spirit, promulgate the truth on matters of faith and morals. We, who had never seen a Council, were inclined to believe that this process would be like the descent of the dove on Christ, a visible pouring out of grace upon those exclaiming at the truth that they beheld and announced.

What did we see? A legislature in action. A legislature with a right, center, and left. A legislature with a variety of committees composing legislation, compromising disputes, considering amendments. A legislature of bishops guided by staffs of experts. A legislature interacting with the executive power possessed by the Pope. A legislature surrounded by lobbyists on every issue.

The conciliar sessions themselves took place in the great basilica of St. Peter, a space suited to the size of the assembly—over 2000 bishops. The side altars of the basilica were turned into coffee bars where over an espresso one could engage in an argument with other participants.

At the end of each day's session there were press conferences, lunches, cocktail parties, dinners. The work of the Council went on not only in the nave of St. Peter, not only in its coffee bars, but around the town—in religious houses, in hotels, in embassies, in Roman congregations, and in the old palace of the Vatican. After the experience of the Council I could not doubt that the work of the Church is done by human beings; that God, whose will we believe was effected by the Council, acts by human means.

That I needed such an experience to grasp how dogmatic truths are formulated shows, perhaps, how easy it is to mythologize if you have not had the experience; to suppose that at some more perfect time divine intervention was more direct and palpable. Now, having had the experience, I am sure that every council of the past, beginning with the Apostles' in Jerusalem, was similar: human beings met, debated, and resolved differences; what was visible was those human interactions. Jean Paul Sartre, in a famous phrase, said that existentialism was humanism. In a much more profound way the Church, shaping its doctrine in councils, is a humanism.

The Development of Moral Doctrine

Secondly, my own work in the history of moral concepts has led to an analogous conclusion as to God's action through human means. I have investigated a variety of moral teachings of the Church—on usury, on contraception, on abortion, on divorce, on bribery, on religious liberty. I have not found that any of these teachings emerged as it were from heaven as a clear and distinct set of commandments. No, these teachings have grown in human soil. They have incorporated pagan perceptions, ancient biology, changing conventions and changing customs. They have maintained, I have written, a central core of values. They have been formulated and developed through human experience. They have evolved.

The prohibition of usury—once defined as any profit on any loan—has been substantially reworked. The prohibition on abortion, once distorted by now discredited biology, has become more stringent. The prohibition of bribery has become more comprehensive. The prohibition of divorce has become affected by new analyses of what makes a marriage. Religious liberty, once denied to heretics, is now prized as a requirement of human nature and the Gospel. God has not entrusted commandments to the Church that are immune from the impact of the increase in knowledge and the impact of changing social conditions. The teachings sit in a human context. The Church, drawing on human experience to form its moral teaching, is a humanism.

The Interpretation of Scripture

Thirdly, I turn to an area that is not my own but which is so fundamental to any understanding of Christianity that it is ignored at one's peril. I mean Scripture. In the last fifty years, beginning with the encyclical *Divino Afflante Spiritu*, this area has been transformed within the Catholic community. The Church, of course, was never a narrowly fundamentalist expositor of Scripture. No person or institution, I believe, can consistently be so. The images and sayings of Scripture are too many, too rich, too contradictory for every image to be taken literally and every text pressed to the letter. How can God be both Banker and Farmer, as the parables suggest? How can Jesus be the perfectly just and therefore unbiased Judge at the Last Judgment and also the Redeemer who has given his life that every soul may be saved from condemnation at that judgment? The multiplicity of images demands discrimination between the meanings intended.

So, too, with the sayings. If your eye offends you, no one supposes that you must obey the words of the Lord to pluck it out. No parent or child takes seriously Jesus' injunction, "Call no man father." No Christian lawyer believes that St. Paul meant him when St. Paul condemned litigation. Texts are controlled by contexts created by the community.

The liberation of the last half century has not, then, been from enslavement to a literal reading of Scripture as standard practice. It has been from an enslavement to a view of Scripture much like that I suggested we held of Councils—a view that the composition of Scripture was by the direct action of God on the pen of the draftsman, a view of Scripture as God's dictation to faithful scribes.

What has come in place of this vision, based on an absence of experience and on lack of close investigation of the text, is the realization that Scripture was written by many hands at many times; that it was assembled and edited before it became Scripture; that it incorporates local conventions, the geography and history of a particular time, the astronomy, biology, and paleontology, now obsolete, of another age; that it responds to particular controversies and is therefore shaped by the context of the particular community to which it is addressed; that it reflects the passions and prejudices of its particular human authors, who were not passive instruments for a divine dictator.

With this change of view of how Scripture was made has come a new freedom in seeing allegory where earlier generations had insisted that there was historical fact as well as allegory. This freedom, to be sure, appears to stop at the pulpit. A chasm presently exists between Catholic scripture studies and the usual Sunday preaching, which affects a literalism in reading the Gospels reminiscent of the old stained glass windows depicting Gospel scenes with exacting detail. We cannot get rid of the pictorial that embodies the literal. But at the level of serious study, a great deal once read as history is now read as theology, an intentional representation by images of a theological insight, written in this style by an author with this theological motivation. Scripture itself is seen humanistically as a human enterprise.

Belief Based on Reason

My general conclusion from these three sets of observations on the operations of a General Council, the development of doctrine about morals, and the interpretation of Scripture: Catholic Christianity is a humanism. But I add at once, it is not only a humanism. It is human action by which God acts. In St. Paul's fine phrase, we are "the co-workers of God" (1 Cor. 3.9).

How do I know? I don't. I believe that God is with us. Belief is not knowledge. It can, however, be based on reason, so that it is neither irrational nor contrary to reason. I turn to the reasons that justify my belief and the counter reasons that militate against it.

First, Catholic Christianity has survived for twenty centuries. It has expanded to every part of the globe. Its survival and expansion prove that it is not culture-dependent. It speaks, and has spoken, to the deepest feelings of millions of human beings. They have found it a home, a friend, a mother, a way of life. If it were not of God, it would have died centuries ago.

This reason may be called the Gamaliel reason after the advice given by the Pharisee Gamaliel to the Sanhedrin as to how to treat the nascent Church: No need to persecute; if it is not of God it will die.

There are two counters to this reason. The first is that the test is not over; who knows if Christianity will last the course? The other is that in fact Christianity has not survived; the name's the same but not the substance. I reject the first objection because it makes Gamaliel's test infinite. I deny the second because I see the constant core.

The second reason for belief is encapsulated in the question the Gospel of John attributes to the disciples: "Lord, to whom shall we go?" If you do not believe in Jesus, in whom will you believe? No spiritual leader has been presented possessing such authority and such love. No doubt in a Western country our culture shapes us, to a degree, to respond to him; but in many ways it blocks or deforms his message. For us at least—let us not speak for others—there are no substitutes as Saviors. And if we do not turn to him we substitute an addiction: alcohol or drugs, sex or work. We cannot tolerate the absence of a god. And if we finally conclude that no god exists, we wander in a darkness painful by the absence of purpose. We turn to Jesus because there is no other person to whom to turn.

The counter-objection, of course, is that the purposeless person may be right. All is chance. No purposes have validity. No god

does exist. Wishing will not change our fate. This objection I
note and pass by. Too much of human striving is purposeful for
any person to ignore purpose and live. Suicide is an option for
the purposeless but not a rational counter to the second reason.

The third reason for belief is the pragmatic reason of Jesus:
"By their fruits you shall know them." What are those fruits? The
art, music, sculpture, and architecture of Europe. The literature of
Europe. The laws of Europe. The hospitals and charitable sodalities of Europe. And beyond all the cultural and social benefac-
tions Catholic Christianity produced persons—for example, to
cite the cultural makers of England from the fifth century to the
nineteenth, its great missionary, Patrick, and its great historian,
Bede; its great political scientist, John of Salisbury, and its great
jurisprudent, Chief Justice William de Ralegh; its great martyr,
Thomas Becket, and its great philosopher, Alexander of Hales;
Geoffrey Chaucer, the poet, and John Bromyard, the preacher;
Lady Margaret Beaufort, the patroness of printing and the two
universities, and William Langland, the moralist; John Fisher,
the martyr-Cardinal, and Thomas More, the martyr-Chancellor;
John Dryden, Alexander Pope and Gerard Hopkins the leading
poets respectively of the seventeenth, eighteenth and nineteenth
centuries; and John Henry Newman, incomparable both as a
writer and as a theologian. What a company to bear witness!

The fruits are also personal. The greatest challenge, the miracle
we all look for, is to move from death to life. With my own eyes
I have seen the physical miracle of prayer making it possible for
my mother, a woman of 87, to survive serious surgery and
recover and to live for years thereafter. I have experienced the
moral miracle of moving from sin to grace hearing the words
of absolution. I have tasted the spiritual miracle of bread becoming the body of the Lord. It is with my own eyes, ears, and
tongue that I have savored the fruits. It is to my heart that the
words of Scripture have spoken. It is I that the sacraments have
renewed. It is to me that the great prayer of the mass has held
out its hope: that we will become co-sharers of divinity, that is,
that our lives will not end with our bodies.

Now I know the answer to this reason: that Christianity has
borne bad fruit as well as good: the Inquisition; the torture, the
burning of heretics; the denial of religious liberty; the degrada-

tion of the Jews; the crusades, the wars of religion, the encouragement of intolerance; the rationalization of slavery; the stiffening of colonialism; the unnecessary intensification of guilt. For every Christian saint or leader there may be a Christian tyrant or traitor. Who but French Catholic theologians and English Catholic soldiers put Joan of Arc to death? The balance of good and bad is at best uncertain.

I must agree that we possess no measuring stick to measure the social goods and ills or the respective weight of good and bad Christians. Weights and measures here are only metaphorical. But one can see the best and know that the worst is the corruption of the best. And in the personal realm no objection occurs which undermines my personal experience of seeing life replace death.

I remain with three reasons: that of Gamaliel, that of the disciples, that of Jesus—reasons, not demonstrative evidence, for believing.

Human Values, Hopes, and Purposes

I do believe as a Catholic Christian that to be a Catholic today means, first, to share many of the values, hopes, and purposes of all other human beings. We are, first of all, part of humanity. Its lot is ours. The Church makes us neither less nor more than human.

From that humanity much, with the aid of historical human experience, may be derived. We share a unity of nature that excludes racism and sexism. We share a rationality that makes coercion of the mind odious and education priceless. We have a need for parents to procreate children and lovingly bring them up. We have a need for governments to protect life and to enhance ways of living. We need values, hopes, and purposes and without them self-destruct with drink or drugs or vice. As human beings we learn to value the truth, to hate cruelty and discrimination, and to love those closest to us and to extend that love ultimately to the alien and the stranger. With experience we formulate the moral laws.

We also know that we must die as inevitably as ants or flies, but we believe that our lives do not end with our bodies. In what that new life consists Scripture does not say except by the vaguest images. "Eye has not seen, ear has not heard," St. Paul tells us. We do not know and despite the speculations of theologians there is little for us to believe. There is a judgment by God—that we believe. Of what concretely follows we have no concept. In the absence of the experience all images and metaphors fail us.

What does the Catholic Church, then, add to our humanity? A direction in reading, thought, and action; a taste or touch of tangible signs; incorporation into a wide and old and exemplary and encouraging company headed by the woman we acknowledge as the mother of God; an encounter with Jesus, man and God, and continued communication with Him; the promise of a judgment beyond time and of a life, real and personal, that goes beyond the grave. Human values, hopes, purposes are confirmed and transcended in that promise which expresses God's love of us.

To be a Catholic in the United States in 1991 is not substantially different from being a Catholic anywhere in 991 or 91, except that the number of companions, past and present, has increased.

The Joys and Responsibilities of Being a Catholic Teacher

Louis Dupré

The news of this award caught me by surprise—the unique joy of suddenly feeling oneself remembered. Remembered by former students after many years, but also by those who read my work. I do not feel that I deserve it. But precisely in receiving without merit consists the beauty of a *gift*. We can only be grateful. And that I am.

In my remarks I shall first speak of the joys of being a Catholic teacher—then of the responsibilities. These responsibilities derive directly from the ideals of a Catholic education. Though each educator committed to those ideals ought to pursue them, in whatever institution of higher learning he or she works, they have become *institutionalized* in a Catholic university such as this. Hence I thought it particularly appropriate to recall, at this joyful occasion, the privilege of actively participating in the pursuit of this most important goal: the formation of human beings with more than human vocation.

Humanitas as an Educational Ideal

One of the most striking innovations of the period we now call "modern" and which, despite our growing reservations about some of its principles, is still our own, consisted in setting up the idea of *humanitas* as an educational ideal. Why should our most common possession—that which we all share, even if we share nothing else, namely, a human nature—suddenly be converted into a moral ideal? The new meaning of the term informs us that henceforth humanity must no longer be taken to be a "given," but a goal to be achieved. Much in that ideal has come to appear questionable to us whom experience has taught to distrust an idea of culture pitted against our *given* nature. But, notwithstanding all misgivings about the concept of self-achievement, one application of that ideal deserves to survive as an almost unqualified good. I am referring to the educational system that emerged from it and that, rather than concentrating on the acquisition of intellectual skills required for performing a specialized task in society, first aims at making the young person a more complete participant in the living cultural tradition in which he or she stands. The educational goal of rendering the student more "human" belongs to the most enviable achievement of our culture.

The Liberal Tradition

Now, actively to participate in the life of one's culture requires an acquaintance with its past accomplishments, the tradition which has shaped its present and must continue to provide guidance for its future. The "Statement on the Catholic and Marianist Identity of the University of Dayton" appropriately defines the task: "The humanities examine the articulations of the meanings humanity has given to its existence, and the importance of history and culture in understanding the nature of tradition and the shaping experiences of the past" (p. 4). Initially the classical segment of that past—the Latin and Greek literature— was considered to hold the essence of all that mattered in our tradition. These days are, of course, long gone—in America even longer than in Western Europe. But what has remained, and what the American college of liberal arts has probably better preserved than the increasingly specialized and professionalized European university, is the concept of a *liberal*—that is the opposite of a *practical*—education as the most appropriate basis not only for a life of learning, but also for a professional, civil service, or business career, or for any other occupation. Among the various duties my own academic work imposes on me, which include such specialized tasks as guiding doctoral candidates, the one I have always favored is that of teaching decidedly non-specialized undergraduates. Here, to my surprise, I feel my own specialized education to bear its richest fruits. In teaching college courses I feel most happy with my avocation as a teacher. While preparing these remarks I chanced upon the testimony of a famous professor of classics at the end of his career:

> I am a teacher. Except for wars and holidays I have never been out of the sound of a school bell. I have written books and given public lectures, but these I have regarded as part of my teaching. The life I lead is the most agreeable I can imagine. I go from my study to a classroom well lighted, comfortably heated, with clean blackboards and fresh chalk, where there await a group of intelligent and curious young men who read the books assigned them with a sense of adventure and discovery, discuss them with zest, and listen appreciatively to explications I may offer. What makes the process most satisfying is the conviction that what goes on in my own and a thousand other classrooms is more important than the large affairs carried on in the shining palaces of aluminum and glass downtown. For I believe that education is mankind's most important enterprise.

Teaching undergraduates is the part of my assignment I shall be most reluctant to relinquish when my time for retirement will arrive. And I find myself nurturing the secret hope that some college or colleges may even then grant me the privilege of occasionally communicating with their young students these riches which do not attain their full substance until they are shared with others. The humanist education has from its inception consisted in conversation. Socrates, Plato, even Aristotle, our ancestors in that education, thought or wrote in dialogue. Renaissance humanists to whom we owe our idea of Humanities polished the art of epistolary communication to perfection. In doing so, Petarch, Salutati, Erasmus, Lipsius followed but the example of their great Latin models, Cicero and Seneca.

Transmission of Spiritual Legacy

As I see it, a liberal education comprises three parts. First, the transmission of that spiritual legacy in which our culture has found its identity and which alone entitles us to consider ourselves full members of that culture. This study of the Humanities in the narrow sense of the term provides the historical erudition about our past, the material substance indispensable for aesthetic education, intellectual training, and moral reflection. That same study also plays a crucial role in achieving the refinement of style and taste which belongs to the essence of all genuine culture. For only an intense exposure to the works of the great poets and writers of the past (and I should add musical compositions, sculptures, and paintings) can educate taste. Nothing less than the voices of the poets will awaken the student to an aesthetic power of words. I vividly remember the unique sensation of pleasure and awe that the simple reading of medieval and Renaissance poems in my high school classes in literature inspired in me when I heard my own language across the centuries articulating feelings that continued to resonate in me.

Human Need to Question

But a genuinely humanist education includes more than historical erudition or aesthetic education. It also responds to what has been called the essentially human "need to question." It requires a thematic and deliberate focusing on those questions which every thoughtful person spontaneously asks. It is, of course, a search that results in more questions than we set out with and that never attains final satisfaction. Each answer reformulates new questions, each partial fulfillment excites new intellectual curiosity. But precisely in that unending search consists the paradoxical satisfaction of the intellectual eros. Socrates implied that the value of a person's life lies in examining it, for only the examined life is the virtuous and hence also the good one. Nor is this the privilege of those who have arrogated to themselves the name "philosophers." According to the Greek sage, it constitutes the value of anyone's life. It includes a training to critical thinking—to acquire the much needed ability to resist the ever subtler deceptions of the age—what Francis Bacon called the idols of marketplace and theater. But it also involves acquiring the methods for thinking clearly. Here the initiation to various positive sciences proves as indispensable as that to philosophy. All too often our students and not infrequently their teachers as well risk to miss much of the purpose of the humanist education as incorporated in the college system by assuming that an option for "humanities" dispenses one from becoming seriously acquainted with the sciences. The opposite occurs, of course, among those choosing the positive sciences. Yet a true humanism knows no two cultures. How could anyone today consider himself fully partaking in the culture of his time while remaining totally ignorant of what must count as the most distinguished accomplishment of our age? Still, critical and methodical thought either in science or philosophy do not define the limits of thinking itself. It has become unfortunately one of the philosophical heresies of our century, especially widespread in the English language territory, that they do, for philosophy also has idols of its own. According to an older tradition the powers of reason must be complemented by the light of the spirit—that light which for St. Augustine comes from above. However we conceive of that intellectual illumination it, and it alone, will place the accomplishments of reason in proper perspective and bestow upon them the unity of thought. This, I think, is the supreme task of philosophy proper, one that is indispensable for attaining the goals of a liberal education. Unfortunately in our day only few colleges, most of them Catholic, have sufficiently resisted the trends either toward an arbitrary freedom of curricular choice or toward a more directly practical education, to maintain philosophy as a required subject. I feel particularly privileged to be honored by one of those select institutions.

Pursuit of Moral Education

Finally there is a third goal liberal education has traditionally set itself, and the pursuit of which has now fallen in almost total desuetude precisely at the time when it has become most needed. I am speaking of the moral education. We who live at the end of the modern epoch have lost our confidence in much of what even the generation of our parents unquestioningly accepted as authoritative principles and rules of conduct. I do not believe that I exaggerate in calling our present age with its unprecedented refusal to accept any restrictions to raw individualism, its general decline of civility, honesty, and respect for life—human and planetary—a period of moral bankruptcy. If there ever was a need for higher education to compensate for what family life and social environment have ceased to provide to the adolescent, it is now. Educating young men and women to think for themselves most decidedly includes an initiation both intellectual and existential into the basic moral principles of a Christian culture. Yet what do we see instead? A general abdication on the part of most colleges of the duty morally to enlighten the young. That the school no longer functions *in loco parentis* does not dispense it from conveying a moral education which consists in more than a relativistic smorgasbord on reports of the choices people actually make and of the various ways in which they theoretically try to rationalize them. Sociology is a legitimate, serious science but no substitute for ethics. The very nature of the tradition into which the educational process must incorporate us has from the beginning posed as its primary principle that the good life is the virtuous one. The Christian assumption of that cultural principle has further explicated it in adding: and the virtuous life is the holy one.

Ethics for the Christian educator ought to be more than information about values. All educational systems are value-oriented, whether they admit it or not. Value consists in what we value, and that may be a very one-sided, subjective ideal. Avoiding a self-centered, or even an exclusively human-centered morality, the Christian looks for an absolute capable of grounding, ordering, and integrating all values. This absolute principle to which the Christian subordinates his entire value system, he or she calls God. Moral education then should be completed by *religious education*. Yet all too often religion itself is presented as adding one more value to all others, thus relativizing what ought to be an absolute ground of values. In functional terms this means that we treat religion as if it were one among many things that we ought to cultivate and learn about. But the "object" of religion does not tolerate this kind of compartmentalization: it either includes all aspects of life or none at all. If God were only the particular subject of an academic discipline called "religious studies" or "theology," He would not be God. Such a discipline is useful and, I think, in a Catholic system of education, indispensable. But the transcendent presence in the educational process touches on all disciplines and, above all, becomes the integrating factor of all moral education. The objective of religious instruction consists not only in communicating the essentials of a doctrinal tradition, but, even more, in assisting the student in extending the religious attitude based on that tradition to all areas of existence.

The Sense of Wonder

Thus religious education should stimulate that sense of wonder and the need to question which we described as the first goals of the educational enterprise. Far form *a priori* defining the purpose and meaning of the historical and aesthetic exploration of our heritage, or of setting boundaries to scientific and critical exploration, a genuinely religious attitude should open the student toward their limitless possibilities and encourage him or her ever further to pursue them. Indeed, religion ought to teach the student to raise questions before it presents definite answers. In no case should it remain satisfied with providing "information" about sacred history, theology, or morals, without rendering that information meaningful, that is, fit to order the theory as well as practice of one's life and to expand their limits. In presenting the human encounter with transcendence, the educator must evoke the fundamental wonder that hides behind all reality, before attempting to define mystery in doctrine (which he also *must* do, and with all the rigor demanded by an academic discipline!)

But religious education will not succeed in its task, neither the general nor the specific, unless it lays in the student the foundations of an interior life, the beginnings of a contemplative attitude. For this purpose some appreciation of silence appears indispensable. Without it the student will be incapable of creating the emptiness needed to be open to faith or, for that matter, to wonder. In silence we take our distance from our surroundings, temporarily suspending the constant summons of the immediate. Perhaps the most valuable contribution of Quaker schools consists in the few minutes of silence that inaugurate each day. Only in silence does genuine prayer originate. I harbor no illusions about the use to which the child or adolescent puts this silence. As one pupil of a Quaker school whom I questioned about the matter, candidly informed me: "We just look around and wait for it to stop." Quite so, but during that short period of mostly boring emptiness everyday meanings cease to be taken for granted. That is why the student feels slightly embarrassed and resists this sudden leave-taking from the familiar world. In silence the student becomes capable of surprise and thus acquires a fundamental openness toward all aspects of life. And, to repeat it, creating such an *openness* should, I believe, be our most immediate objective in Catholic education. Without it we must abandon all hope of establishing any authentically religious or selflessly moral attitude.

The Interior Self

True interiority, far from enclosing the person within himself, should liberate him from the manifold cares and petty desires that obstruct his way to the other. The cord of the interior self consists not in a concentrated point of self-identity, but precisely in a relation to otherness. Genuine interiority results in uninhibited communication. This appears paradoxical only because of our unfortunate habit, itself typical of the modern attitude, to oppose self-hood to otherness. A less subjectivist concept would reveal selfhood to be total openness. The social achievements of the great masters of the interior life confirm this conclusion. Who was more feminine, both in affection and in effectiveness, than Teresa of Avila or Catherine of Siena? Who more influential as a leader of men than Ignatius of Loyola? Who socially more engaging than Francis of Assisi? Yet precisely they are remembered as the great masters of spiritual life! Even the highly speculative Eckhart served as a remarkably efficient superior of the Rhineland province of the Dominicans, in addition to being a successful preacher. In his well-known sermon "Blessed are the Poor" he admonishes his audience that to be genuinely poor the self must deprive itself from everything, including its own identity. "If one wants to be truly poor, he must be as free from his creature will as when he had not been born." What is this but total openness expressed in unrestricted availability to the Other, to others?

Gratitude and Respect

To conclude this reflection on a concrete note, allow me to mention two virtues that signal and promote interior openness: gratitude and respect. Essentially religious in nature they also form the basis of a refined moral sensitivity. Gratitude is the active counterpart of wonder. In teaching his or her pupils not to take the benefits of life for granted and to be grateful for what it offers, the Christian educator may well make his or her most specifically religious contribution in the moral field. In gratitude we abandon the standpoint of our own private needs and affirm our dependence with respect to the other. We cease to take ourselves as the center of existence and allow the Other or the others to be *what they are.* Gratitude actively reaches out to the other, regardless of personal feelings or desires. As such it sets the primary condition for any kind of spiritual life, and indeed, for Christian love itself. For to love in the Christian sense I must first forsake my attitude of possessiveness toward the other, and love the other for his or her own sake. Gratitude is the virtue that all devout women and men share. The Buddhist as well as the Benedictine monk *thanks* all day long, independently of his personal mood or feeling. He thanks because it is morning, noon, or evening. At the end of the day he sings his thanks for whatever the day has brought—pleasure, boredom, or pain. How he "feels" has no effect upon his thanksgiving: every day is God-given and, as such, good.

Together with gratitude, and partly as a result of it, Christian education should create and foster the virtue of *respect,* possibly the most neglected quality in the moral habits of our time. Only if we accept the other on his or her terms are we capable of respect. To respect the other is precisely not to draw him into the closed circle of my own subjectivity, but to encounter him in the open space where he is allowed to be himself.

You may consider the preceding suggestions marginal with respect to the more fundamental issue of the specifically moral and *religious* quality of our education. I fully admit that they are preliminary to a moral education and even more so to an initiation into the Christian faith. Yet marginal they are not. Because as a precondition for its success a genuinely Christian education demands a radical reversal in attitude. Without such a change the word will not be heard, and, if heard, will not be understood. The religious educator needs as much re-education as the student needs an education, for he or she is often as much affected by the self-centered, pragmatist heresy of our age as those entrusted to his or her care. In this state of affairs our immediate concern should first go to the disposition itself within which religious faith may take root. Allow me to summarize this preparatory task in words which I wrote some years ago:

> What is needed is a conversion to an attitude in which existing is more than taking, acting more than making, meaning more than function—an attitude in which there is enough leisure for wonder and enough detachment for transcendence. Culture requires freedom, but freedom requires spiritual space to act, play, and dream in. [. . .] The space for freedom is created by transcendence. What is needed most of all is an attitude in which transcendence *can be recognized again. (Transcendent Selfhood: The Loss and Rediscovery of the Inner Life.* New York: Seabury Press, 1976, p.17.)

A Catholic Scholar's Journey through the Twentieth Century

Monika K. Hellwig

We are graced to live in a century in which both the world and the church have been going through significant evolutionary changes at lightning speed. The full meaning and impact of these changes will only be apparent in retrospect, and we who are here today may no longer be alive to understand what was happening in the world and church of our time, but our attempts to see the signs of the times with the eyes of gospel faith will be not only a response of gratitude to God, a kind of contemporary *Magnificat*, but also a gift of wisdom to those who come after us.

Such a reading of the signs of the times and of the redemptive grace being dispensed in them is necessarily rather like a jigsaw puzzle in which each of us holds certain of the pieces which will make up the picture only when joined with the others. All biography is of this nature, and autobiography gives a certain depth and immediacy of meaning which is a great gift to others but only becomes entirely trustworthy when it achieves balance in complementarity with the stories of others. It is with this hope and this caution that I offer you a retrospective on the twentieth century church and its world as I have known them. If I offer some personal details from my own life, it is so that you may know just where the observer was standing who saw what I

71

relate, and what was the personal experience and formation that shaped the interpretation of what was seen.

The Early Years

I was born in Breslau, in Silesia—an area then part of Germany, in December 1929. Germany was suffering terribly from the great depression (though my immediate family was comfortably placed), and a few months later, in 1930, Hitler's German National Socialist Workers' Party (Nazis for short) won a great election victory. When I was three years old, Hitler became Chancellor of Germany and within a year he had consolidated his power by having police and other forces under his direct personal control, giving him power to murder all his political opponents by mid-1934, and to become the unchallengeable dictator (under the euphemism of "leader") when President von Hindenburg died in August of that year. By 1935 when we moved to Berlin in pursuit of my father's career as an economist, Germany had become a place of fear and tension among intellectuals, professionals, artists and families such as mine which had a wholly or partly Jewish background. When my father was killed that Christmas, many of my relatives were already fleeing Germany, and my artist mother took her three children to Limburg, the southernmost province of the Netherlands. This was where I was standing as a child observer of church and world of that time.

My parents had grown up in World War I and its terrible aftermath for Germany. They spoke little about this, but they were not optimistic about the politics of Germany or its potential at that time for genuine democracy. And where was the church? As we children experienced it, the church remained quite snugly within the church buildings, and these were places of impressive silence, mysterious activities, and a time of respite from the activities of the world—the ubiquitous sound of marching feet, the Heil Hitler salutes, the crowds always ready to explode into hysteria, and the furtive glances of many pedestrians. The church did not seem to enter into this world but to provide a haven from it.

Perhaps this impression on a child's mind was not altogether wrong. It is true that Pope Pius XI and his nuncio, Eugenio Pacelli (later Pope Pius XII) faced the double jeopardy of the rightist dictatorships and the bolshevik left, and seem to have seen the latter as the greater threat. It is also true that some church leaders spoke out boldly against the persecution of the Jews, notable among them being Msgr. von Galen and Cardinal Faulhaber. Many priests, such as Jesuits Delp and Mayer, offered active resistance, as did some unsung heroes and heroines among the laity. This last was due at least in part to hierarchic sponsoring of Catholic Action in many parts of Europe, and certainly also to the dynamic writings and lectures for the laity of such men as Karl Adam, Peter Lippert, and Romano Guardini; not to mention the serious study of social and economic issues by dedicated Catholic scholars. But when all is said and done such initiatives did not represent the mainstream life of the church. For most Catholics (and probably for most clergy and hierarchs) hope related rather exclusively to a goal after death, and was supported by exercises of piety and the observance of the commandments in one's daily life.

At the same time, the church in the English-speaking world was not challenged in quite the same way. Because of the pattern of migrations, the English-speaking Catholic churches tended to be the faith communities and cultural homes of workers, often building solidarity through parochial schools and through the institutional support of workers' rights. In the U.S. the Great Depression added to the need for charitable activities on the part of the institutional church, and in the wake of the "Americanism" controversy, concern over orthodoxy seems to have outweighed concern over such major issues as racial discrimination. In any case, threats such as faced Europe between Hitler and Mussolini on one side and Stalin on the other, did not affect the English-speaking countries internally.

Peasant Catholicism

Europe was a cauldron of oppression coming to the boiling point and its churches were in need of the greatest wisdom and subtlety in discerning how to intervene, and of heroic courage in taking the appropriate actions. The vicissitudes of my family, however, transported us into a still eye of the storm where a very different kind of Catholicism survived. My father's Catholicism had been that of the intellectuals. My mother's, dating from her adult conversion, had been stamped with the Benedictine tradition with its focus on Bible, liturgy and continuity with traditions of Christian life, thought and spirituality. The Catholicism of Limburg in the southern Netherlands was peasant Catholicism of a vigorous and cheerful kind. It was inclusive of all aspects of human existence, and splendidly sure of itself, leaving no room for doubts or questions. I consider it a great gift and privilege to have known peasant Catholicism; it is the fertile soil out of which the church grew for many centuries.

In the pattern of village life, the church's calendar ruled everything. For the sacred Triduum of Holy Week, everything stopped, and everyone participated in the services. On Easter Sunday everyone went to church twice and wore new and festive clothes, probably spending the rest of the day visiting one another. On Corpus Christi everything stopped for the great procession which wound its way through every street and lane of the neighborhood, so that every house could be blessed with the Blessed Sacrament displayed in the monstrance. Those houses would have been cleaned and scrubbed inside and out, and decorated with flowers and banners. Christmas meant the whole village lit up and decorated, everyone coming to midnight mass, usually through the snow, and returning for a daytime mass in the morning. School children especially, but in some measure all the villagers, lived the cycle, of the feasts and seasons of Christ's life as naturally as they breathed the air of the place. We were part of that cycle, it was our life, and the village was populated with opposing forces of angels and devils as distinctly as though we had seen them with our bodily eyes.

But it was not only the liturgical cycle that embraced us. We were also caught up in the festivals of the saints. St. Martin was a local patron, and on his feast there were great celebrations in a meadow near the village—a bonfire, games, distribution of treats for the children. And into the midst of it, riding on a great cart horse from one of the farms, came St. Martin in military cloak, accosted by a most miserable and pathetic beggar (homeless people and beggars being a phenomenon we knew only from fairy tales). We children would be jumping up and down with excitement, waiting for the dramatic moment when the great sword was drawn and the cloak slashed in two to be shared with the beggar. There were similar celebrations of saints' days, but most vivid of all was the Shrove Tuesday parade in which a good deal of audio-visual catechetical instruction was conducted live in the streets of the village. There were floats representing many biblical stories, sometimes a drama enacted in its entirety, and always a wonderful representation of hell, complete with devils bearing tridents. All Souls' Day saw everyone attending three masses and then visiting the cemetery, bearing late blooming flowers or greens.

Not only was all our time sacred time, but all our space was sacred space. Houses were furnished with statues and holy water, people wore scapulars and medals, and village and wayside were dotted with little shrines. My mother, who was a sculptress, found that her madonnas were very much at home here because Mary, the Mother of Jesus, was a member of everyone's family in this culture. We were all part of the household of God, in which some were already gathered about the throne in heaven and the rest were on their way there, either in purgatory or on earth, but it was all really one extended family. Knowing the catechism was one of the Catholic obligations, but it was not really the way one learned the meaning of the faith: that was learned from life because it permeated the whole culture.

Catholicism in England and Scotland

There was only one way in which this apparently invulnerable worldview could come to an end—by external forces destroying the society and its culture. That happened with World War II, but I was not there to witness it: what I saw next was the Irish Catholicism represented in Scottish and English boarding schools. By 1939 it was clear that the Netherlands were by no means safe from Nazi occupation. My mother was unable to get a visa to any safe country for herself and her parents, but by May of that year we children found ourselves in boarding school in Edinburgh, Scotland. The world as seen from a convent boarding school of that time was violent, dangerous, but (except for intermittent air-raids) far away from this haven of literature, learning and the peacefulness of an orderly life framed in regular structure of prayer. In the war and immediate postwar years, in boarding schools and sometimes in hospitable family homes of English and Scottish people, a new type of Catholicism came into my ken.

It soon became clear that there were two quite distinct types of Catholics in Britain: there were the old English families that had maintained their Catholic allegiance through times of persecution and terror, through ridicule and exile, discrimination and poverty. They were mainly old families of landed gentry, who had sent their children overseas to be educated and had until recently led a rather secluded life on their country estates. Some of their tenants might also have remained Catholic through the times of persecution. To these were often added other English families, often scholars or people distinguished in public service with continental connections. Such Catholics were reserved, well informed, careful in ritual observances, emotionally restrained in their devotional style, conservative in theological and church questions, and extremely private about their faith. Later, when the Second Vatican Council took place, many of them felt somewhat betrayed. There were aspects of Catholicism for which some of their ancestors, whom they could still identify by name, had died—such as the Latin Mass, the observance of fast and abstinence days, the veneration of saints and images, and particularly Marian devotion—all of which now seemed to be devalued. These old English Catholics and their Scottish counterparts were often highly educated and cultured people, and there was among them a serious tradition of private spiritual reading and of spiritual direction. Their sons often became Benedictines, Jesuits or Dominicans. Their daughters might become Benedictines, Religious of the Sacred Heart, Ursulines or Mary Ward Sisters. They tended to be quite class-conscious. Although they were certainly involved in many types of charitable activity, there is little evidence that they were moved to protest social injustices, towards the Irish for instance, or towards the subject peoples of the British Empire.

The other type of Catholic in England was Irish interspersed with some Italians and with Second World War additions of

Poles and others. The Irish Catholics in England were much more numerous and more evident, tended to be less educated, less reserved, less private about their devotions and perhaps also less critically aware of what was central and what was peripheral. The Irish Catholics of England and Scotland seemed more dependent on their parish clergy. They too carried vivid remembrances of persecution, but these were intimately entangled with the national question and therefore tended to evoke a more belligerent stance on behalf of Catholicism. The sons of the Irish Catholics were more likely to be found in the diocesan seminaries and among the diocesan clergy of England than in the older religious orders, and their daughters were more likely to be Mercy Sisters or members of other newer communities, especially those that maintained close ties with Ireland. In the parishes, of course, the two types of British Catholics mixed, but always with some awkwardness and discomfort over the style of religious expression in art, music, participation in worship (such as it was in those days of passive attendance).

University Years

Such were my observations growing up in Britain in those years. In retrospect I think they were by and large correct. It was when I began university studies in 1946 that I began to have some experience of what it was that kept the Catholic intellectual life in existence in Britain. I studied at one of the newer universities, often referred to as the "red brick universities" to distinguish them from those that traced their history to the middle ages, and therefore boasted dignified grey stone buildings. It was not only the brick that distinguished us: whereas the older universities had strong ties with the established church (the Church of England or of Scotland respectively), the newer universities had a very anti-religious (not specifically anti-Catholic) bias. It was feared by the bishops and their advisers that young Catholics attending these universities were in great danger of losing their faith. Something rather different happened. Most of us who gained admission to the universities had had excellent religious instruction in our high schools, and were keenly critical of any caricatures of religion presented to us. We took the attitude of our professors as an intellectual challenge calling for vigorous and well informed counterattack.

In any case, the bishops and the religious orders in collaboration identified some of the best scholars and teachers among their priests, and assigned them to be university chaplains. These chaplaincies were not permitted to take office on university property, but generally rented space nearby so that students could have easy access. Besides the social events calculated to encourage marriages within the Catholic community, and the liturgies and retreats to sustain the spiritual life of the students, theological lectures were a very important part of the work of the chaplaincies. Excellent lecture and discussion series were organized, and often guest lecturers were brought in. This was by no means something that was imposed on the students from above. The undergraduates had long held the status of a club registered in the student union with the privilege of booking rooms and so forth. We ourselves, those of us who were keen to do it, often requested a series of lectures and found the lecturers. We had series on the modern social encyclicals of the popes, on particularly troublesome historical issues, and particularly on scholastic philosophy and theology. We were still in those years of the late forties in a mode of thinking about Catholicism, which focused on continuity with medieval achievements and tended to see all modern developments as oppositional to the faith. Hence we would arm ourselves intellectually against our philosophy professors and some of our history professors at the university. We were quite sure, and our elders encouraged us in the conviction, that by attempting a coherent and foolproof scholastic philosophical synthesis of our twentieth century lives and learning we were the hope of the future.

It was not surprising that we should have seen our Catholic intellectual identity in this way. The Modernist crisis was only a few decades behind us, Catholics in the universities still considered themselves in a state of siege, the theology of seminaries and religious scholasticates was still totally dominated by the aftermath of the Council of Trent, and we were proud of our certainties. It was, however, in the context of literary and historical discussions that some of the Catholic intellectuals who held teaching positions at the university found the freedom to think more broadly about the modern world, and some of us were privileged to belong to essay clubs in which such reflections were shared by small numbers of professors and students in a range of disciplines. Moreover, our horizons were necessarily broadened by exchanges in the student union where the Marxist Society was one of our favorite sparring partners, and where debating and drama were frequent and absorbing activities.

Catholic Truth Society

Having graduated in law and subsequently in social science/ social service, I found that in the working world religion became extremely private again, but I continued to read and study theology. A great institution of the Catholic Church in Britain in those days was the Catholic Truth Society, which did two things: it published books and pamphlets, and it held courses and public debates in Hyde Park in London. Such lively minds as C.C. Martindale, S.J., Frank Sheed, Maisie Ward, Frederick Copleston, S.J., Douglas Hyde and Vincent McNabb, O.P., were involved in this. From the lectures and public debates they had a good sense of the questions on the minds of thinking Catholics and others who might be interested in Catholicism. They left no stone unturned to find the most appropriate authors—authors who both understood Catholic theology and tradition thoroughly and were also able to express it in brief pamphlets and nontechnical language. Most churches had pamphlet racks in the entry hall well stocked with the Catholic Truth Society publications, and from them any avid and intelligent reader could gain a good theological education.

Frank Sheed and Maisie Ward did more than publish pamphlets and speak at Hyde Park Corner. They themselves studied and wrote and eagerly recruited Catholic writers—novelists, essayists, historians, biographers and so forth. Moreover, they acquainted themselves with the continental Catholic writers and scholars and commissioned translations of Maritain, Guardini, Blondel and others. While Sheed & Ward in those days tended to look for the new, the firm of Burns & Oates continued to publish the old stand-bys—nineteenth century sermons and lives of Christ, traditional books of devotion and so forth.

With all this reading available, and the provision of public lectures, I found that I had qute an extensive theological education through informal channels long before I began formal theological studies at the Catholic University of America in 1955. Moreover, there was another very important intellectually formative experience for young people in those days. Encouraged by the success of the Jociste Movement on the continent, the English Jesuits, notably Fathers Bernard Bassett and Peter Blake, had begun to revive the sodalities of Jesuit educational history, under the name of the Cell Movement. It involved small groups which met on a regular basis, and annual national gatherings at the seashore for a week. Intended to encourage lay people to take an active role in the world about them to promote Christian values, the meetings included rather extensive study of, and meditation upon, the Gospels. This was in a context in which it was still rather unusual for Catholics to do any private Bible reading. In the course of these meetings I became very familiar with the New Testament, though there was still no stimulus to read it in the light of the Hebrew Scriptures. It was when someone gave me a copy of the Jerusalem Bible in French (when it first came out), that the Bible as such was opened for me. I spent much time tracking down the marginal cross references, and slowly learned to recognize the allusions and to grasp some of the symbolism. I have the impression that someone with no other resource than the large edition of the Jerusalem Bible, complete with marginal cross references, could come to a very sound grasp of the Bible and of biblical interpretation.

Another formative influence for me in these years was an introduction through a friend to the writings of a Dom Columba Marmion. In them I found the deeper theological interpretation of what I had experienced in the peasant Catholicism of Limburg. The pattern of the liturgical year as a frame for contemporary lives, the importance of symbolic stories and actions, and the wealth of role models all fell into place, broadening my sense of what theology was and how it functioned, from the narrow constraints of the scholastic model to a wider humanistic range.

American Catholicism

When I came to know the Catholic Church of the United States, in the mid-fifties, it was as a student of theology at the Catholic

University of America in Washington, D.C. After my earlier experiences of university studies in a secular, and even anti-religious environment, the Catholic University of America was a strange experience—on the one hand a sense of having come home intellectually, but on the other hand a sense of being intellectually cramped. I was amazed, for instance, that the philosophical background we were expected to have as students of theology totally excluded all of modern thought. Even though, as I noted before, we Catholic students of the British universities had some ideal and not clearly defined scholastic philosophical synthesis in mind as desirable, we had in fact assimilated and somehow integrated the modern philosphy and social sciences we had read. Its absence in the theological scene as presented to us at that time at Catholic University was something I felt keenly, the more so as the Index of forbidden books had not swum across my ken before. At that time at the Catholic University the constraints of the Index were so earnestly and literally observed that not only the clearly anti-religious or seductively heterodox books were locked in wire cages where students would have no access, but such books as the translation of Romano Guardini's *The Lord* had found their way into the cages only because the translator or publisher had chosen an unauthorized translation for the biblical quotations.

Something else that I found amazing and distressing at this time was the lack of preparation of the priests who were my classmates in the M.A. and Ph.D. programs. I had not at that time had much experience of seminaries and seminary curricula and textbooks on either side of the Atlantic, and had always supposed that while we lay intellectuals who read theology purely out of interest were, so to speak, the beggars at the gate, that seminarians for whom the study of theology was a full time occupation were being provided rich fare so that they could continue and sustain the Catholic intellectual tradition. Why I should have thought this I do not know, because I had certainly heard many inadequate sermons, shallow retreat conferences, and inane conversations, but somehow I had thought that behind this was a depth of genuine theological reflection and wisdom that was not being shared with us. During that year of M.A. studies in the fifties it first began to dawn on me that the vocation to priestly ministry does not necessarily carry with it intellectual curiosity or studious inclination, and that ordination does not confer wisdom or intellectual maturity. Moreover, it began to be clear to me that if the tradition with all its wonderful intellectual history and content was to be sustained, brought into contact with the modern world, and enriched by new syntheses, the laity could not wait passively for this to happen in clerical circles.

That year and in the years that followed I began to see how this might come about. I was teaching during the year, getting exposure to a wide range of American parishes across the country, and attending the summer sessions of the Summer School of Liturgy at Notre Dame University. The experience of the parishes at that time gave me a sense of how hard the American Catholics were trying to look American, and Catholics leaping with enthusiasm into the McCarthy era of Communist hunting. They were neither political like the continental European Catholics, nor simply enclosed in their own world like the peasant Catholics, nor yet were they discreetly private like the old Catholic familes of England, or provocatively flaunting their difference like the Irish Catholics of England. They were trying to line up Catholic and U.S. ideals in the hope that they could be shown to be almost identical. This struck me so forcefully because of the contrast with the scholarly and creative reflection that I was hearing in the Notre Dame summer sessions. With generous endowments from the Grace shipping line, Michael Mathis was bringing from Europe many of the great scholars who were the forerunners of the Second Vatican Council in their thought— Bouyer, Danielou, Luykx, Bouman, Jungmann, Goldbrunner, Vitry and others, unfolding for us biblical scholarship, patristics, liturgical history and theology, the deeper meaning of the Gregorian chant and its link with the liturgical cycle, ecclesiology and the theology of pastoral ministry, new thought about missions, and much more. These summer sessions were a meeting of many cultures, and a window to the future of the churches. They opened doors to a more ecumenical pattern of reflection, and they gave the much needed historical perspective. It was during these years that I made the acquaintance of Godfrey Diekmann, a great teacher, who opened patristic literature and liturgical theology for countless number of adult Catholics who would later teach others. I also maintained contact with Gerard

Sloyan who had been one of my professors in the MA program and who had introduced existential and historical dimensions into the study of the New Testament at a time when it was generally taught in a quite uncontextual way.

Second Vatican Council

With this background of observation of local churches in Europe and America I came in the early sixties into contact with the universal church at the Second Vatican Council. By a gracious dispensation of providence I was in Rome, first to ghost-write a book for an official at the Holy See, and then to help give retreats at the International Pius XII Centre of the Movement for a Better World. At the press conferences those who were fortunate enough to get tickets could hear Rahner, Schillebeeckx, Ratzinger (then very much in the theological vanguard), Kung, and many others among the periti explain the issues being presented to the Council and the reasons for their urgency or importance. Those of us who read Italian could actually follow the speeches day by day in the *Osservatore Romano*. This experience of the universal church awakening and speaking and taking note of the challenges of the modern world on all sides was an intellectually and spiritually intoxicating experience. I found that it vindicated so much that had seemed to be in tune with the gospel but had been held at bay by the guardians of orthodoxy. It was spoken of at that time as a new Pentecost, and it certainly was a new birth of the Church in the contemporary world.

Return to Washington

Soon after the Second Vatican Council, I returned to the Catholic University of America, at the invitation of Gerard Sloyan who had always been a devoted talent scout for budding theologians. It is to him that I chiefly owe my subsequent career as a theologian because I had at the same time an invitation to return to my alma mater in England to teach the history of political philosophy, and without the assistantship in Washington I should certainly have remained in Europe, reading theology only as a personal interest and private sideline. Subsequent reflection has made me very sympathetic to conservative factions in the Church who found the post-conciliar changes intolerable. Had I returned to England, I would have been greatly enriched by the wider sense of Catholicism from my travels and greatly enlightened by the experience of the Council, but I would not have gone through the arduous, lengthy and sometimes painful process of rethinking my appropriation of my Catholic heritage, because I would not have had the leisure to do so, the easy access to wiser and older people going through the same process, and the advantage of being well guided in my reading.

The second stay at the Catholic University was wholly unlike the first. Theological courses for the academic (as distinct from the pontifical) degrees were packed with graduate students, very many of them layfolk, many of them no longer young, who were in search of the new fountains of the old wisdom from the centuries, now that the floodgates had been opened. The student body in these graduate courses organized a lively liturgical and social life, so that it became an experience of church in a prophetic and visionary mode. The teaching of theology, largely under the guidance of Sloyan (who was doing the hiring), took on a problem-solving style, rather than a simply indicative or imperative one. It took on three-dimensional depth from the historical approach in which the shifting of perspectives and emphases, the raising of new questions through the ages and consequent changing shape of the project, and the debates that shaped the teaching at various times in the past, became evident. With this, of course, came the realization that all our theology is reflection on the praxis of our lives as Christians, and that all the official teaching of the church is the product of a communal discernment of the appropriateness of what emerges from the theological reflection on experience. To revisit the arguments and reflections of the past is a very privileged opportunity to serve an apprenticeship in the process of building our tradition. Because we live in the twentieth century that tradition is rich in literature, iconography, philosophy, spiritual traditions, liturgical forms, devotional options and patterns, as well as informal theology. It is a precious heritage and a very great responsibility entrusted to those of us with opportunity and leisure to read and reflect, to study and teach.

Why do I write, coming from such experience of the church and such opportunities to observe and study? Mainly because so many others with the potential to appropriate their faith in an intelligent and creative way do not have the opportunities that I have had, but also because I realize more and more what a delicate process of discernment is involved in judging what are the new insights that will truly enrich the old tradition and keep it to the gospel vision of world and redemption. Iconoclasm lurks ever at the door and in the corners of our awareness, and the function of the new is not to destroy but to fulfill. Many interested and intelligent Catholics of our time are given very little help in making those discernments.

What I Have Learned

In my journey through the twentieth century as a Catholic scholar, what have I really learned? First of all, that we cannot keep the Holy Spirit out of the church, no matter how much we try to domesticate the whole enterprise. Secondly, that the church is wiser and more faithful when it listens discerningly to many voices, even those from outside its own boundaries. Thirdly, that we, all of us, are the bearers of tradition and the shapers of it for the future, and that we have immense wealth entrusted to us. Fourthly, never to be afraid of the truth, but to seek truth with humility and faith and the readiness to be proved wrong and to begin the search again. Fifthly, that conflict is part of growth and the shaping of tradition, but that hatred and rejection of those who differ need not be. And lastly, that as educated Catholics of our time we are part of a very important intellectual contribution to our society and to the world—a contribution that is an integral component of the redemption.

What Made Catholic Identity a Problem?

PHILIP GLEASON

Receiving the Marianist Award for 1994 is a very great honor and a mark of recognition for which I am deeply grateful.

It is an honor not merely in itself but also because it allows me to claim fellowship with the distinguished group of Catholic scholars whom you have chosen for the award in past years.

In that group, I am especially gratified to find myself associated with two other historians—the late Monsignor John Tracy Ellis (1986) and the Honorable John T. Noonan (1991)—whose work I admire enormously and both of whom I am proud to call friends (although in the case of Monsignor Ellis that friendship is now but a cherished memory).

I might add that being placed on a plane of equality with the provost of my own university—Timothy O'Meara, who won the award in 1988—can hardly prove disadvantageous to me back in South Bend.

I feel especially honored also in being the first alumnus of UD to receive the award since it was reactivated in the mid-80s. It is, I have to admit, a long time since I graduated in 1951, but I have the fondest recollections of my undergraduate years.

I like to think that Brother Louis Faerber, who encouraged my interest in teaching in those distant days, would take some satisfaction in this award. And I don't doubt that Brother William O. Wehrle, who exercised a benign despotism over the third floor of Alumni Hall dormitory, would feel considerable surprise at what is going on here.

Not that I ever caused the good brother any trouble you understand. And in fact I remember him, not just as a disciplinarian, but as the teacher of a course on the history of the English language that was one of the most interesting of my prolonged career as a student.

There were many other memorable courses—Richard Baker's history of philosophy, William Canning's US history survey, Erving Beauregard's Expansion of Europe (where I learned that Norway has a longer coastline than the continent of Africa), Kathleen Whetro's American literature course (where I learned what "venery" means), and Wilfred Steiner's medieval history course for which I read a book that contained an unforgettable line—one that is applicable in many situations of life and learning. It comes from the prologue to Robert the Monk's history of the First Crusade and runs as follows: "The more studiously anyone directs his attention to this subject, the more fully will the convolutions of his brain expand and the greater will be his stupefaction."[1]

That isn't the text for my talk this afternoon because I don't really want to stupefy you. I do, however, hope to expand the convolutions of your brains just a bit in connection with the question that does furnish my text: "What made Catholic identity a problem?"

The question, of course, refers to the Catholic identity of Catholic colleges and universities. That is a hot question now—at least at Notre Dame—and has been for quite a while. I want to talk about it from two angles: from the perspective of one whose memories (as you just learned) go back to the late 1940s; and also from the perspective of one who has studied the history of Catholic higher education in the 20th century. These two dimensions have become so intermingled that I honestly couldn't say which has been most important in shaping my present understanding of the subject.[2]

Catholic Identity at Mid-Century

Considered from the vantage point of the present, the most striking thing about the Catholic identity issue in the 1940s and

1950s is that it didn't exist. The reality, of course, existed—existed in the sense that Catholic colleges and universities definitely *had* that identity, *were* Catholic, and made no bones about *professing* their Catholicity. What didn't exist was the "problem" of Catholic identity. That didn't exist because the Catholicity of the institution was so much of a given—seemed so obviously a fact of nature—that no one regarded it as a problem any more than they regarded it as a problem that a college was a college and not a filling station or a furniture factory.

In other words, the Catholic identity of places like the University of Dayton was a reality that could be taken for granted—and was, indeed, taken for granted. But there was a kind of paradox here, for the main reason Catholic colleges of that era could be unself-consciously Catholic was that Catholics were still self-consciously "different." That is, American Catholics were so conscious of holding distinctive *religious beliefs* that it seemed perfectly obvious that they needed their own schools to perpetuate the outlook on life that flowed from those beliefs.

So long as Catholics continued to constitute that kind of distinctive religious subculture, the Catholic identity of Catholic colleges would not emerge as a problem. For as the historian of religious change at Amherst College wrote, "The very acceptance of an idea operates to make exegesis needless and apology supererogatory. Only when its validity is challenged will there appear a body of definition and discussion."[3] The challenges that eventually started people talking about the "problem" of Catholic identity were only beginning to take shape at midcentury. They were still much weaker than the internal and external factors reinforcing that identity as a given quality whose existence could be taken for granted.

The chief internal factor reinforcing it was the continuing momentum of self-confidence produced by several decades of fabulous growth in numbers of faithful, in organizational energy, and in spiritual vitality. The Catholic intellectual revival of the interwar period—called by some the Catholic Renaissance—carried over strongly into the post-World War II era. So did the various apostolic movements inspired by what was known at the time as "Catholic Action" (of which Dayton's Father Ferree was a major theorist). The closely related battle against "secularism," which had gotten under way in the thirties, reached its climax in the late forties. Thinkers like Jacques Maritain and John Courtney Murray, S.J., gained a respectful hearing for the Catholic tradition in philosophy and theology; on a less rarefied level, journalists like John Cogley applied natural-law reasoning to the problems of the day. Catholicism attracted intellectual converts, and Thomas Merton's *Seven Storey Mountain* (1948)—the story of his conversion and vocation to the priesthood as a Trappist monk—became a minor publishing sensation. Monsignor Fulton J. Sheen, who was a famous convert maker, reached a wider audience as a lecturer, spiritual writer, and media personality.

In a word, the American Catholic subculture seemed to be in good shape intellectually speaking. It was plagued by no doubts about having a distinctive religio-intellectual tradition, about the contents of the tradition, or about the responsibility that fell on Catholic colleges and universities to articulate the tradition, present it to young people, and represent it in the larger world of learning.

Externally, the religious identity of the Catholic college was reinforced by certain features of the national cultural scene. The war had sparked a revival of religion, for there were, as the saying had it, "no atheists in foxholes." On a deeper level, totalitarianism and war discredited secular liberal ideas of human perfectibility and rehabilitated "Christian realism." That expression was particularly identified with Reinhold Niebuhr, who infused his influential social and political commentary with the spirit of Protestant Neo-Orthodoxy. By the late 1940s, observers were calling attention to evidence of a major "revival of religion." That, along with the country's Cold War repudiation of Communism, was well calculated to bolster the morale of Catholic educators and reinforce their commitment to integrating faith and learning in their colleges and universities.

Counter-Currents

At the same time, however, counter-currents were beginning to build up that would at length render problematic the hitherto taken-for-granted quality of these institutions' Catholic identity. The subtlest was the continuing social assimilation of the Catholic population, and the concomitant acceleration of the process by which Catholic colleges and universities adjusted themselves to prevailing standards in the larger world of American higher education (especially after they took up graduate work in earnest). This twofold process of social and academic acculturation took place gradually and—especially in respect to social assimilation—more or less beneath the surface. For that reason it went unnoticed for quite some time. Indeed, it was not until the 1960s that social scientists began to publicize the finding that Catholics had experienced dramatic upward mobility and by then surpassed their Protestant fellow citizens "in most aspects of status."[4]

As they became less distinguishable from other Americans in terms of income, occupation, residential location (for they, too, moved to the suburbs), and educational aspiration—and as the sense of ethnic distinctiveness faded for the grandchildren of immigrants—Catholics, especially the young people who came of age after World War II, began to wonder whether they were so different from everyone else that they had to have their own separate institutions, and why they were expected to hold different views from other people on matters such as divorce and birth control.

The earliest indication of this tendency was the intra-Catholic criticism of "Catholic separatism," "ghettoism," and the "siege mentality" that erupted around 1950 and continued strongly for several years. No doubt it was in part a response to hostile external criticism. For while the Catholic critics defended the Church from foes like Paul Blanshard, who portrayed Catholicism as intrinsically unAmerican, they also wanted to eliminate whatever features of Catholic life gave needless offense to others. This made good sense in the highly charged atmosphere of interreligious conflict over issues like aid to parochial schools, which Protestants and secular liberals regarded as examples of arrogant "aggressiveness" on the part of Catholics. To defuse this kind of hostility, Catholic liberals urged their coreligionists to participate more actively in "the mainstream of American life" by joining "pluralistic" movements for social betterment along with Protestants, Jews, and non-believers.

The advice was perfectly justifiable in the circumstances, but it was also inevitably assimilationist in tendency. Insofar as it was assimilationist, criticism of "ghettoism" implicitly endorsed the underlying social processes that were making Catholics more like other Americans and simultaneously weakening their distinctive identity. But even if this had been pointed out at the time, the critics would probably have dismissed it as unimportant. For they were objecting to what they considered unduly exaggerated forms of Catholic distinctiveness. Catholicity as such, they would have said, was far too deeply rooted to be at all threatened by eliminating these extremes.

Self-Criticism

This view of the situation was implicit in the most famous critique of American Catholic academic performance ever published - Monsignor Ellis' "American Catholics and the Intellectual Life," which was published in 1955 and set off a chain reaction of "self-criticism" that continued into the early 1960s.[5] Ellis' target was not ghettoism as such, but the lamentably weak showing made by American Catholics in scientific research, scholarly publication, and intellectual leadership generally—all of which of course reflected very unfavorably on Catholic institutions of higher education. Ellis did, however, hit hard at ghettoism in his conclusion, which was that Catholic scholars' indolence and their "frequently self-imposed ghetto mentality" were primarily responsible for this dismal record.

But despite his unsparing criticism, despite his coming down hard on ghettoism, and despite his urging Catholics to "mingle" more freely with "their non-Catholic colleagues," it was quite evident that Ellis regarded the Catholicity of Catholic scholarship as being too deeply rooted to be in any way threatened by a public airing of its deficiencies or by closer association with outsiders. On the contrary, it was only by following his counsel that Catholic scholars could "measure up" to their responsibilities as bearers of "the oldest, wisest and most sublime tradition of learning that the world has ever known."[6]

But as the chorus of self-criticism mounted in the late fifties, much else besides laziness and ghettoism was causally linked to "Catholic anti-intellectualism." Thomas F. O'Dea, for example, identified formalism, authoritarianism, clericalism, moralism, and defensiveness, as the five "basic characteristics of the American Catholic milieu which inhibit the development of mature intellectual activity." And Daniel Callahan carried the logic of criticism to its seemingly inevitable conclusion by announcing that "the real culprit" was "the American Catholic mentality" itself.[7] At this point, one might reasonably have asked whether Catholics had any solid basis for thinking they had an intellectual tradition that was even respectable, much less one that was "the oldest, wisest, and most sublime" in the history of the world.

A Challenge to Identity

Though self-criticism was thus intended as an assault on Catholic smugness—which did, indeed, furnish a very large target—it could not help but raise deeper questions about the content of the Catholic intellectual tradition. That in turn posed an implicit challenge to the identity of Catholic institutions of higher education, for it was their ostensible dedication to that tradition that gave them their distinctive character.

Increasingly sharp criticism of Neoscholastic philosophy had the same effect, since it had previously been considered the intellectual centerpiece of the Catholic Renaissance and the most essential element in the undergraduate curriculum. By the late fifties, however, Catholic educators had largely abandoned their earlier preoccupation with "integrating the curriculum" around a core of Neoscholastic philosophy and theology. Instead, they devoted themselves to the "pursuit of excellence"—with excellence being understood as the way things were done at places like Harvard and Berkeley.

Of course, most professors in Catholic colleges were too much absorbed in "their own work" to keep abreast of the Catholic intellectualism discussion, or to pay much attention to curricular developments that did not impinge directly on the self-interest of their departments. But they were being affected by more subtle changes. One such change was heralded by growing opposition among Catholic sociologists to the older view that there was such a thing as "Catholic sociology."

This was significant because sociology was different from

mathematics or chemistry. No one had ever prescribed "Catholic" approaches to those subjects; but the founders of the American Catholic Sociological Society insisted that their discipline was different because the teacher/researcher's personal worldview and value commitments entered directly into the way sociology was studied and taught. The fact that a new generation of Catholic practitioners regarded the "Catholic sociology" approach as outmoded and embarrassingly parochial reflected a degree of academic acculturation that foreshadowed more pervasive identity problems to come.[8]

Those problems were to burst forth in the 1960s, but they did not do so right away. Pope John XXIII, who issued his call for *aggiornamento* in 1959, and John F. Kennedy, who was elected president the following year, seemed the bellwethers of a new and better day for an American Catholicism that had "come of age" (to use a phrase popular at the time). Indeed, the last of the strictly Ellis-inspired "self-critics" veered dangerously close to a new kind of smugness by asserting that, thanks largely to the younger lay professors who had absorbed "professional standards" in graduate school, Catholic colleges were in "transition from a prolonged intellectual adolescence to a point where they can face the challenges of maturity."[9]

By that time (1964), the pace of *aggiornamento* had picked up so markedly that the same author, John D. Donovan, could refer to "fundamental challenges to the validity and viability of the theological, structural, and historic warrants of the pre-1950 system" of Catholic higher education.[10] But this abstract and stuffily academic way of putting the point corresponded to the muffled and obscure state of the question at that time. The "fundamental challenges" were still latent. No one—or at least no Catholic— had come right out and said in plain language that just as there could be no such thing as "Catholic sociology" neither could there be such a thing as a "Catholic university."

What precipitated that crucial next step, raising the issue in the starkest terms and causing it to be stated with brutal directness, was the explosion over academic freedom set off in December 1965, when St. John's University in New York summarily dismissed thirty-one professors. In the aftermath of that gross violation of academic due process, and as other academic freedom cases erupted (including a much-publicized case here at UD), George Bernard Shaw's dictum that a Catholic university is a contradiction in terms was quoted repeatedly, and John Cogley, the erstwhile promoter of natural law, said a Catholic university was as outmoded as the papal states. But the unkindest cut, which was also the most revealing of changing attitudes, came from two Catholic professors at Fordham (one a layman, the other a priest) who said that urging people to take up an "intellectual apostolate"—a staple of earlier "self-criticism"— was tantamount to recruiting "holy panderer(s) for the Catholic Church."[11]

A Crisis of Confidence

Catholic intellectuals—and therefore Catholic institutions of higher education as well—were obviously undergoing a severe crisis of confidence. A generation earlier, this would have been called a "failure of nerve"; by the mid-sixties, people spoke instead of "identity crises." At Notre Dame (to which I went as a graduate student in 1953, joining the faculty six years later) the identity problem did not emerge directly from the uproar over academic freedom, although we did stage the first scholarly symposium on the subject ever held at a Catholic institution.[12] Notre Dame's awakening to the academic identity problem as such was a byproduct of the more general identity problem that overtook American Catholicism after Vatican II. And that, in turn, took place against the background of the national crisis of confidence caused by racial violence, antiwar protests, and campus disturbances. Adding to the social and political turmoil were unsettling shifts on the cultural front, most notably the drug-saturated "counterculture" and the women's liberation movement.

The religious identity of Catholic colleges and universities thus emerged as an explicitly recognized *problem* when three powerful forces came together in the mid-1960s. The first of these was the social and educational assimilation of American Catholics that had been building up since World War II. Besides making them think and feel more like their non-Catholic neighbors, this progressive acculturation had been accompanied by self-criticism that made Catholic academics positively ashamed of the past and determined to break out of its mold.

How long it would have taken for these internal pressures to bring the Catholic identity issue to explicit formulation is a moot question, for the other two forces—Vatican II and the national cultural crisis of the sixties—intervened. In combination they popped the cork on the pent-up internal forces and multiplied the shattering effect of the resulting explosion. Their influence was especially marked in reinforcing and generalizing the tendency to *reject the past* that was already present as an element of the situation created by the internal pressures. *Change* was the talismanic word in those days. The past, as I heard the president of a Catholic women's college say, was irrelevant because the future would be entirely different!

Obviously this was not the only reaction to the Council and the domestic upheaval, but it was of crucial importance for our topic. Why? Because the Catholic identity of Catholic colleges and universities was an inheritance of the past, and in the postconciliar climate that made it an *ipso facto* candidate for change. How could it remain a taken-for-granted assumption—an unselfconsciously held and therefore unexamined given—when everything else in Catholic belief and practice was being scrutinized, challenged to justify itself, reinterpreted, modified, or even rejected? That their religious identity would now become an explicit problem was made even more inevitable by the fact that the colleges had been subjected to so much preconciliar criticism for weaknesses said to flow from clericalism, authoritarianism, and other characteristics associated with their being Catholic.

The emergence of the problem did not, of course, mean that those who discussed it—even those highly critical of the past— wanted Catholic colleges and universities to reject or abandon their religious identity. Outright secularization was an extreme option recommended by very few and followed by even fewer. The great majority of Catholic educators wanted their schools to remain Catholic. At the same time, however, they realized that "being Catholic" in the future could not be exactly what it had been in the past. For two reasons: because the self-understanding of the Church as a whole had been transformed by the Council, and because on-going changes in Catholic higher education itself had reached a tipping point that required some fundamental readjustments.

The Catholic Identity Problem

Thus the Catholic identity problem was (and is) precisely that—a problem. It is a problem because, though Catholic identity is prized as something to be cherished, nurtured, and preserved, neither its substantive content nor the means to be employed in maintaining it are anything like as clear as they were in the preconciliar era. For we must remember that it was the clarity of Catholic religious beliefs in the 1940s—and the conviction that the Church would "never change her teaching"— that made the Catholic identity of Catholic colleges a taken-for-granted given. After Vatican II, when the Church's teaching had undeniably been changed, Catholic belief was not nearly so clear as it had been. How then could Catholic educators continue to take for granted what was no longer there as a given?

If the problem "surfaced" (as people used to say in the sixties) roughly three decades ago, how has it developed since then? That is too obvious a question to ignore, but too big a one to try to answer. Let me conclude with a few informal comments based mainly on what has happened at Notre Dame.

First, it is striking how much attention the subject has received. Thus when the new lay board of trustees took over its duties in 1967, the revised by-laws of the university included an explicit commitment to maintain Notre Dame's Catholic character and that commitment has remained an active concern of the board ever since. Each of the three major university self-studies since the early 1970s has also placed preserving Notre Dame's religious identity first among institutional priorities. And the issue has been discussed in many other campus forums over the years.

The prominence of the issue flows naturally from the shift from its being something that could be taken for granted to something that needs to be self-consciously articulated. Hence the discussion seems to me not only appropriate, but vitally necessary. Even the disagreement that the discussion causes, potentially damaging to the internal harmony of the university community though it be, at least shows that the matter is being taken seriously.

The disagreement itself flows from the two sources mentioned above: the transformation of the Church's self-understanding wrought by Vatican II and subsequent developments; and ongoing changes internal to Catholic colleges and universities. Illustrative of the first are differences between conservative and liberal Catholics over issues like academic freedom, theological dissent, the role of the magisterium, the relation of colleges and universities (especially the latter) to ecclesiastical authority, and the degree to which "education for justice" can serve as the core element in an institution's Catholic identity.

Faculty Changes

Among on-going internal developments bearing on the Catholic identity issue the most important, in my opinion, are changes in the composition of the faculties of Catholic colleges and universities. Thirty years ago, Donovan drew attention to changes in outlook and orientation accompanying the growth of the lay faculties whose younger members were mainly recruited from leading "secular" graduate schools. The shifts he sketched have become more noticeable in recent years. Priests and religious have virtually disappeared as a numerically significant factor on many faculties, and no longer dominate the ranks of academic administrators as they used to.

Even more significant, however, is the operation of a generational transition that has all but completely displaced faculty members (lay and religious) whose outlook was formed when the earlier mentality held sway. Not all of the older generation were equally articulate about or committed to maintaining the religious character of their institutions, but it is a fair generalization that a good many more of them were so disposed than is the case with the generation that has replaced them. In addition, many of these younger faculty members consider it unprofessional—indeed, highly improper—to take a candidate's religion into account as a consideration in hiring. As a Jesuit writer has observed, by 1970 it had become "declasse" to show any interest in that dimension of a candidate's background.[13]

The growth of this kind of feeling among faculty members, along with the disagreements already mentioned about what "Catholic identity" entails in substantive terms, adds up to a serious problem indeed. And its seriousness is heightened by the fact that over-reaction to it, especially on the part of ecclesiastical authorities who feel an understandable concern for the future of Catholic colleges and universities, could easily make matters worse instead of better. Continued discussion is of course necessary for, as I have already said, what can no longer be taken for granted has to be raised to a new level of self-consciousness and articulated in more explicit terms.

It will not be easy for all parties to that discussion to combine the requisite degree of clarity and frankness with the equally essential qualities of moderation and—perhaps most important of all—respect for the good will of the opposition. For despite the depth of feeling involved, the suspicions aroused, and the polemics that too often accompany exchanges on the subject, there is, I believe, a great reservoir of good will still shared by all the parties to the discussion. Being a historian, I would like to think that the reservoir of good will is fed, at least in part, by the realization that what is at stake is the continuity of a tradition venerable in age, rich in humane associations, and honorable in its achievements, which it is our obligation to hand on in the form best suited to future needs.

Notes

1. Dana C. Munro, *The Kingdom of the Crusaders* (New York, 1936), 174.

2. For more detail on what follows, see my chapter, "American Catholic Higher Education, 1940–1990: The Ideological Dimension," in George M. Marsden and Bradley J. Longfield, eds., *The Secularization of the Academy* (New York, 1992), 234–58.

3. Thomas LeDuc, *Piety and Intellect at Amberst College, 1865–1912* (New York, 1946), vii.

4. Norval D. Glenn and Ruth Hyland, "Religious Preference and Worldly Success: Some Evidence from National Surveys," *American Sociological Review* 32 (February 1967), 73–85.

5. John Tracy Ellis, "American Catholics and the Intellectual Life," *Thought* 30 (Autumn 1955), 351–88.

6. Ellis, "American Catholics and Intellectual Life," 386–88.

7. Thomas F. O'Dea, *American Catholic Dilemma* (New York, 1958), chap. 7; Daniel Callahan, *The Mind of the Catholic Layman* (New York, 1963), 98.

8. For more on this shift see Philip Gleason, *Keeping the Faith* (Notre Dame IN, 1987), 67–70; and the articles in the Fiftieth Anniversary issue of *Sociological Analysis* (vol. 50, no. 4, 1989).

9. John D. Donovan, *The Academic Man in the Catholic College* (New York, 1964), 193. The study on which this book was based was the last one commissioned by the Catholic Commission on Intellectual and Cultural Affairs as a follow-up to Ellis' critique.

10. Donovan, *Academic Man*, 195.

11. John Cogley, "The Future of an Illusion," *Commonweal* 86 (June 2, 1967), 310–16; Edward Wakin and Joseph F. Scheuer, *The De-Romanization of the American Catholic Church* (New York, 1966), 261.

12. See Edward Manier and John W. Houck, eds., *Academic Freedom in the Catholic University* (Notre Dame IN, 1967).

13. Joseph A. Tetlow, S J., "The Jesuits' Mission in Higher Education: Perspectives and Contexts," *Studies in the Spirituality of Jesuits* 15–16 (November 1983–January 1984), 33.

The Church in the World: Responding to the Call of the Council

J. Bryan Hehir

This lecture is an expression of gratitude to the University of Dayton for the 1995 Marianist Award. There is much for which to be grateful: the intrinsic purpose of the award; the privilege of being associated with the previous honorees, all of whom I have had the privilege of knowing personally; and the personal respect I have for your President and your Provost, both of whom are playing crucial roles in the contemporary dialogue about American Catholic higher education.

The tradition of this lecture invites the speaker to address a substantive issue in Catholic life and to relate it to his or her own intellectual history and professional work. The topic I have chosen, "The Church in the World: Responding to the Call of the Council," allows me to focus upon a significant anniversary in post-conciliar Catholicism and to incorporate personal reflections as well. The year 1995 marks the thirtieth anniversary of the final document of Vatican II, *Gaudium et Spes* ("The Pastoral Constitution on the Church in the Modern World").[1] This text is the church's most recent authoritative address to a question which is as ancient as the New Testament and as contemporary as today's *New York Times*. For it addresses the issue of how the church of Christ understands its place in history, how it defines its posture in relationship to secular institutions and how it speaks, by word and example, to the principal political, economic and social issues of the day. Christ framed the question by instructing his disciples to be responsive to both God and Caesar, but the nature of his teaching and the example of his life provided a challenging body of resources to determine how to fulfill his command with fidelity and integrity. Throughout Christian history the concise but deceptively complex dictum of the Master has left disciples with open-ended questions about both the church and the world.

Vatican II's response, framed in the middle of the twentieth century, echoes earlier answers in the Catholic tradition but moves beyond them. In terms of its content and the catalytic role it has played in the life of the church since 1965, *Gaudium et Spes* already stands as a monumental text. The purpose of this lecture is to provide a sense of the historic significance of the last and longest document of Vatican II. In doing so, it will be a simple task to provide a personal dimension since this text has had a defining impact on my academic work and ministry in public affairs on behalf of the church. It is also the case that the basic direction of my theological teaching and writing has been heavily influenced by individuals whose research provided the foundation on which *Gaudium et Spes* rests. They are all part of that remarkable corps of theologians, born at the beginning of the century, whose work climaxed in Vatican II.

To capture both the significance of the conciliar achievement and to illustrate the role of the theology which shaped it, I propose in this lecture to analyze the church-world question in three steps: first, a statement of the central role it has played in Catholic history; second, an evaluation of the background, content and consequences of *Gaudium et Spes*; and third, a sketch of illustrative issues engaging church and world in the 1990s here in the United States.

Church and World: History and Structure of the Question

The pervasive presence of "the world" in the New Testament and the contrasting evaluations given of it guaranteed the church-world question a central place in the history of the church.

The scriptures generated more questions than they answered; it was the task of the tradition to grapple with the problem opened by Christ's dictum about God and Caesar. The references to the world cut across a variety of New Testament texts. St. Luke locates the birth of Christ and the ministry of the Baptist securely in the context of the Roman Empire. All the evangelists place the crucifixion in the context of the ongoing tension between the Jewish leadership and the Empire. St. John's gospel depends heavily on the statement that "God loved the world so much that he gave his only Son" (Jn. 3:16), yet the Son ends his life reminding the disciples that "They are strangers to the world" (Jn. 17:16), and I John warns them not to set their hearts "on the godless world or anything in it" (I Jn. 1:15). St. Paul's theology of history depicts the whole cosmos awaiting redemption ("...the universe itself is to be freed from the shackles of mortality and enter upon the liberty and splendour of the children of God." Rom. 8:21), but he warns the disciples not to be conformed to the pattern of this world (Rom. 12:2).

The inherent tensions of the biblical texts provided precisely the kind of question which is addressed in the Catholic tradition through systematic theology. The church-world question has been posed at two levels: the conscience and choices of each disciple and the role of the church in history. The responses to the church-world question are woven through the entire history of Catholic theology, beginning with the patristic literature and extending through the pontificate of John Paul II. Augustine structured the argument in classical fashion with his "two cities" doctrine, traces of which are still evident in *Gaudium et Spes*. Also evident is the influence of Aquinas' more positive conception of the state and civil society derived from his fusion of Aristotelean political philosophy and the Christian gospel. The power of Augustine's conception of sin, grace and history and Aquinas' sense of the dual resources of reason and faith will be part of any Catholic understanding of the church-world problem. But neither the Roman Empire nor the medieval *Respublica Christiana* exhausted the range of problems and possibilities which secular institutions could pose for the church as a community and a social institution. Neither Augustine nor Aquinas had to grapple with the rise of the nation state (secular in character and concentrated in its power), the shattering impact of the Reformation, the transforming scientific power of the Enlightenment, the emergence of democratic polity, the positive and negative effects of the Industrial Revolution. By the nineteenth century the church was in need of a fundamental recasting of the church-world question, something which would approximate in scope and depth the work of an Augustine. For most of the century the response of the church was timid and inadequate; it faced fundamental change by retreat and reaction. Renewal came with the pontificate of Leo XIII (1878–1903) who inaugurated three fundamental reforms in Catholic life: intellectual, social and political.

Intellectually, he launched the Neo-Scholastic revival of philosophy and theology with St. Thomas Aquinas as the patron of the movement; this initiative decisively shaped Catholic thinking and teaching through the middle of the twentieth century, including the work of Jacques Maritain, Etienne Gilson and many authors in the Catholic social tradition. Socially, Leo XIII grasped the challenge posed for the church by the impoverishment of the working classes in Europe and North America; his response, *Rerum Novarum* (1891), the first of the social encyclicals, established a papal tradition of highly visible engagement with socioeconomic issues throughout the century. While later encyclicals moved beyond Leo XIII's thought on a number of questions the dominant note of the encyclicals is one of evolutionary development. Politically, Leo XIII devoted a substantial corpus of writing to issues of church-state relations, even as he also reinvigorated the diplomatic role of the Holy See in world affairs. The dynamic of development in Catholic thought on church and state moved quite beyond Leo XIII, but not until the teaching of Vatican II. When development occurred, the break was sharper on church-state than on the social issues.

Taken together these three dimensions of Leo XIII's pontificate made a major contribution to the church's role in the modern world. Leo XIII was a transitional figure; that judgment can be made at the end of the twentieth century. But for two-thirds of this century his teaching set the basic structure for his successors.

To trace the lines of continuity and change which have occurred since Leo XIII, it is not sufficient to analyze "the social teaching" in an undifferentiated manner. The scope and quantity of Catholic teaching about the church's place in society and its relationships with the structures of secular life require some distinctions: church-world, church-society and church-state. The church-world question, the principal focus of this lecture, is the properly theological understanding of the church's role in history. The argument is cast in theological terms: sin and grace; ecclesiology and eschatology; ethics and anthropology. The church-world question is the framework within which the church-society and church-state issues are developed. The church-society statements, primarily the papal social encyclicals from Leo XIII through John Paul II, seek to relate Catholic moral tradition to a range of socio-economic issues, first within nations and then on a global basis.[2] The church-state arguments are cast in political-juridical terms, relating Catholic theological ideas to the changing structure of the state in different historical periods. The church-state teaching, principally found in Leo XIII, Pius XII, Vatican II and John Paul II, builds upon the church-world premises but it is more institutional in character.[3]

This three-dimensional view of Catholic teaching provides a way of thinking about the church's relationship to the *world* as a cosmic and historical reality, to *civil society* in its social, economic and cultural dimensions, and to the *state* as the center of political authority in society. Vatican II's teaching engaged all three levels of Catholic thought, but its major impact was on the church-world question.

The Conciliar Text: Background, Content, and Consequences

The sources of the teaching varied in the first half of the twentieth century. The church-society and church-state themes were developed primarily through papal writings. The church-world issues were the stuff of theological discourse and research.

Except for Pius XI's encyclical on the kingship of Christ, *Quas Primas*, papal teaching did not contribute substantially to the theology of church and world. Pius XII's discourses and messages about the apostolate of the laity and his far-reaching contributions in *Mystici Corporis* and *Mediator Dei* provided impetus to the theological work addressing the church-world question directly.

The theological writing was both extensive and creative; it was part of a broader process of fundamental theological research which led directly to the Second Vatican Council. While the architects of this theological renewal had no sense that an ecumenical council was just over the horizon, in retrospect we can see the direct and substantial connection between the theology of the 1930s through the 1950s and the documents of Vatican II. The theological work cut across biblical and patristic research, ecclesiology and ecumenism, liturgy and social teaching.

In the midst of these themes, the church-world question held a special status: it was intrinsically important, but it also served as a catalyst for the way in which other theological topics were approached. The principal architects of the broader theological renewal saw the church-world issues as the horizon in light of which specific aspects of theological research would be pursued. Henri de Lubac, the French Jesuit, whose life and work in this period exemplified the vitality and vision of pre-conciliar French Catholicism, focused his research on overcoming a "separated theology" pursued apart from the major intellectual and social currents of the day.[4] Yves Congar, the French Dominican, whose life and work complemented that of de Lubac, described the way in which their theology was shaped by a sense of responsibility for the church-world question:

> I cannot exaggerate the importance of the new consciousness which theologians have acquired of their responsibility to the church and to the internal credibility of the faith which the church must offer mankind.[5]

On a personal note, it was Congar who served as my introduction to the church-world questions. I had by nature, family influences and study a clear orientation to social and political issues by the time I entered seminary. While I had a general sense of the social significance of Christian faith, it was by reading Congar's *Lay People in the Church* in my first year of seminary that I encountered a qualitatively new level of understanding of the church's teaching and its role in society. Congar, de Lubac and their Jesuit and Dominican colleagues were pursuing a two-tiered research agenda, engaging the most pressing contemporary political, social and cultural issues, and seeking to respond to them from the biblical, patristic and liturgical sources of the faith. Joseph Komanchak, analyzing the dynamic of de Lubac's research, also describes the spirit of the theological enterprise leading to Vatican II:

> It was an attempt to recover a Christianity intellectually rich and spiritually powerful enough to be impatient with the marginal role with which too many theologians had become content and to be eager to exercise a redemptive role in all of human life.[6]

Describing even minimally the scope and substance of this theological project is a task which exceeds this lecture; it would have to encompass the work of prolific authors like Marie-Dominique Chenu, O.P., Jean Danielou, S.J., and the Belgian priest Gustave Thils. All contributed original research on the church-world question as did Karl Rahner, S.J., and Edward Schillebeeckx, O.P., writing in a different theological style from the French Jesuits and Dominicans. All that is possible here is a snapshot of how these theologians established a foundation for Vatican II's decisive contribution to the church-world question.[7]

Henri de Lubac, seeking both to overcome a "separated theology" and to share with the church and the world an "intellectually rich and spiritually powerful" Christian vision, produced in 1938 a fundamental interpretation of Catholic faith in his book *Catholicism: A Study of the Corporate Destiny of Mankind*. De Lubac's basic concern in this book which evolved from a series of essays was to demonstrate the *essentially* social character of Catholicism. In one sense the motivating force of the book is apologetic, because it seeks to refute a conception of Christian faith as inherently individualist and inevitably isolated from the larger issues of society and history. One can feel de Lubac's visceral and intellectual reaction to such a view of faith in his introduction to *Catholicism:*

> We are accused of being individualists even in spite of ourselves, by the logic of our faith, whereas in reality Catholicism is essentially social. It is social in the deepest sense of the word: not merely in its applications in the field of natural institutions but

first and foremost in itself, in the heart of its mystery, in the essence of its dogma.[8]

De Lubac's commentary, appearing almost fifty years after the first social encyclical, is obviously intended to go well beyond the claim that the church has a social concern and a social teaching. He seeks in *Catholicism* to illustrate the social nature of this faith in two ways. First, to show the social character of Catholicism as expressed in its sacramental life, its conception of community and its doctrine. Secondly, to illustrate how the intrinsically social nature of the church in turn produces a perspective on history, the meaning of the person and the theory of society which places Catholicism at the center of the world and its quest for unity at the spiritual, social and political levels of life. Far from being individualist and escapist in character, de Lubac understood the church to be deeply engaged in a quest for unity which is rooted in human nature, but brought to a new level of meaning and solidarity by faith:

> Humanity is one, organically one by its divine structure; it is the Church's mission to reveal to man that pristine unity that they have lost, to restore and complete it.[9]

For de Lubac the faith and the church *are* social before they articulate a response to social needs and social questions. His conception of both Christian faith and the Catholic church established a foundation for the church-world question which is reflected in the opening paragraph of *Gaudium et Spes*:

> The joys and the hopes, the griefs and the anxieties of the men of this age, especially those who are poor or in any way afflicted, these too are the joys and hopes, the griefs and anxieties of the followers of Christ. Indeed nothing genuinely human fails to raise an echo in their hearts. . . . That is why this community realizes that it is truly and intimately linked with mankind and its history.[10]

Foundations, however, need to be elaborated in terms of a structural framework. It is this which Yves Congar provided in his study of ecclesiology and eschatology. In *Lay People in the*

Church, Congar explores the history of the church-world question in Catholicism in terms of the key structural concepts of church, kingdom and history. Drawing on the work of Thils, as well as the contrary view of Louis Bouyer, Congar provided both a summary of the church-world debate and a statement of his own position. He begins with a lucid and comprehensive definition of the question:

> Many are preoccupied by this question today, and it is approached sometimes as the theology of history, sometimes as the theology of earthly things. The problem is to know whether what we do in the secular sphere of this world is altogether irrelevant and without importance for what will be the kingdom of God.... Education, increase of knowledge, advance in techniques and methods of production, use of the world's resources, development of our physical bodies—has all that a relationship, some continuity, with the final reality of God's kingdom? And if so, what?[11]

While acknowledging the permanent validity and presence in the community of the church of what Congar calls "the dualist-eschatological view," as expressed in the monastic vocation's search for conformity "with the City that is to come," he finds more convincing as a basic position for the church, "a certain continuity between the human work of this world on the one side and the kingdom of God on the other...."[12] Congar takes care to distinguish his position from Thils and others who, in his view, collapse the distinctions among church, world, and kingdom too easily. But the differences between Congar and Thils are a matter of degree. They both advocate a transformative view of ecclesiology and eschatology: the kingdom ultimately is a work of the Spirit, a gift of God, but the Spirit transforms what has been prepared in history by human work through culture, scholarship, politics, art, economics and law.

The structure which Congar provides for the church-world problem leads directly toward *Gaudium et Spes.* While the conciliar text will manifest the fifteen years of theological work between *Lay People in the Church* and *Gaudium et Spes,* Congar's basic design of the problem remains. The kingdom is both present in history and transcends history: it is within us and ahead of us. The created world, while ambivalent and ambiguous in terms of its orientation toward the kingdom because of sin, provides the raw material for the heavenly Jerusalem. The work of human intelligence and creativity which perfects the created order points toward the culmination of history in the eschaton—hence the lasting value of human work. Both the church and world are destined for the kingdom, both serve the purposes of the kingdom but using different means and with different purposes in the overall design of God. Without denying the legitimate autonomy of secular society and history, Congar sees the church's ministry in terms of directing the world toward the kingdom:

> The Church is the direct preparation for the kingdom, having within herself the strength of the Holy Spirit, and she cannot but strive to transform the world to the utmost. Of necessity she seeks as much as possible to reduce the evil in the world, to rebuild it in good order, to make operative the healing, uplifting, transforming force of which we have spoken above, the gifts of grace.[13]

Both the foundational theology and the framework (ecclesiological and eschatological) of the church-world question in the twentieth-century were given their critical impetus in European theology. But the framework sets the stage for the next level of reflection, the specific forms of relationships which should exist between the church and the secular institutions. While Congar, de Lubac and others addressed this issue productively, the most important single contribution came from the American Jesuit, John Courtney Murray, a contemporary of the European theologians, whose sure grasp of the intersection of theology, law and politics allowed him to recast the church-society-state relationships in a way that moved beyond both Leo XIII and Pius XII.

Murray's work, pursued over twenty years prior to Vatican II, involved a double dynamic. Convinced that the nineteenth-century formulation of the church-society-state question prevented the church from engaging democratic theory and practice, imprisoned it in a debate which had been superceded by changes in the secular world and, thereby, distracted it from the larger task of renewing its witness in the world, Murray first had to relativize the authority of nineteenth-century papal teaching on state and society. He then had to construct from the resources of the Catholic tradition and his understanding of contemporary political theory a conception of church-society-state relations for this century and beyond. To accomplish both tasks he used a sophisticated blend of theology and history. He reviewed the tradition with great respect, in search of "transtemporal" structural principles which are rooted in the nature of the church and society, but always reminding his audience that the principles assume multiple forms in different historical periods.[14] Drawing on diverse authorities reaching across the span of Catholic history (Popes Gelasius and Gregory VII; Jean of Paris and Pius XII) Murray culled a set of principles which should structure the church's relationship with the institutions of the world. They included respect for the distinct origins, purposes and methods of church and state; defense of the principle of freedom of the church from secular dominance; respect for the primacy of spiritual values, combined with the need for collaboration between church and state; and acceptance of religious pluralism as the context of the church's ministry. Use of these principles would allow the church to shape the church-world problem in a way which placed the church in defense of human dignity and human rights, and in a position to serve civil society without being subordinated to secular power.[15]

This sketch of theological research prior to Vatican II conveys a sense of a time of profound change and development in Catholic thought. Part of the narrative, told well in other sources, is the fact that those doing the basic research were severely burdened in their work by a pattern of suspicion, restriction and repression which affected most of the key contributors to Vatican II. Rather than detail this history, my focus must remain on the relationship between the theological work summarized thus far and the product of Vatican II on church and world. The relationship can be defined in two ways: the conciliar text *Gaudium et Spes* is dependent upon and emerges from the theology of the previous thirty years; but it also surpasses the earlier work, having its own distinctive character which could not have been simply predicted from the research prior to the council.

Gaudium et Spes moves beyond previous writing on the church-world question because of its synthetic quality. The text draws on both the resources of Catholic social teaching and the theological

work which we have surveyed in this lecture. The major contribution of the text lies in Part I which is the explicitly theological
section of *Gaudium et Spes*. Part II resembles the social encyclicals,
and, while it makes important contributions in its chapters on
marriage and on international relations, the innovative character
of the document remains the ecclesiological vision of Part I. In
a council centered on the church, *Gaudium et Spes* adds a decisive
chapter to Catholic ecclesiology.

The synthetic quality of the text resides in the way in which
ecclesiology is located within a broader theological argument.
Part I joins theological anthropology, eschatology and ecclesiology. The conciliar text locates the church *in* the world. From a
nineteenth-century posture which placed the church *against* the
world, this text moves even beyond a conception of the church
and the world to one in which the world in its cosmic and historical dimensions is the starting point for theological reflection.
After reviewing the "signs of the times" which characterize the
world of our time, the council locates the church in the midst
of the world as "a sacrament of unity," an active agent of unity
in human history. The location of the church then raises the
question of how the church should fulfill its unifying ministry.
The answer of Vatican II is that the distinctive mark of the
church's ministry should be its capacity for dialogue with the
world in its multiple dimensions. The dialogue, as Fr. Congar
notes in his commentary in *Gaudium et Spes*, is not that of a
teacher and a pupil; reciprocity must mark the church-world
dialogue since the church has something to learn and something
to teach about the topics raised in Part II of *Gaudium et Spes*.[16]
One way in which the conciliar text fosters reciprocity is the
clear recognition of the intrinsic value and validity of secular
institutions and secular disciplines. In affirming the role and
value of secular institutions, *Gaudium et Spes* is complemented
and deepened by *Dignitatis Humanae* ("The Declaration on Religious Freedom"). Both texts led the church to acknowledge the
legitimate autonomy of the world; this respect for legitimate
secularity is shown by the council's regard for the secular character of the state, its respect for the established methods of research
in various fields of knowledge and its recognition that effective
dialogue means speaking in terms which secular audiences can

grasp. Productive dialogue, therefore, requires a pastoral strategy based upon recognition of and respect for the secular context of the world in which the church finds itself.

Gaudium et Spes is not content, however, simply to locate the church in the world and sustain a dialogue about issues affecting both church and world. The conciliar text seeks to give its answer to the church-world problem summarized above by Fr. Congar. To some degree Gaudium et Spes is a response to the theological debate about church-world themes which had been underway for thirty years. Congar had classified one response as a dualist-eschatology, one which stressed a sharp break between the results of human effort and the final gift of the kingdom which would be purely and simply a work of the Spirit. I characterized Congar's own position as a transformative view in which a close connection exists between ecclesiology and eschatology, and the final product of the kingdom is a result of human effort consecrated and transformed by the work of the Spirit.

In light of this background, it is clear that Gaudium et Spes opts for the transformative model. While there is a clear warning in the text that human progress should not be confused with the growth of the kingdom, at a deeper level the teaching of Vatican II affirms the lasting significance of human work, culture, science and politics viewed from the perspective of faith:

> For after we have obeyed the Lord, and in His Spirit nurtured on earth the value of human dignity, brotherhood and freedom, and indeed all the good fruits of our nature and enterprise, we will find them again, but freed of stain, burnished and transfigured.[17]

While the council's statement lays stress on the continuity of human effort and divine intervention, the theology of Gaudium et Spes is not a unilateral affirmation that the kingdom of God is a human creature. The structure of the conciliar argument is anthropological in its foundation, eschatological in its culmination, ecclesiological in its focus and christological in its content.

Congar's commentary on Gaudium et Spes argues that the shift in the church-world question manifested in the council is a move from a political-juridical conception of the church's role in the world to an anthropological perspective.[18] The person is the link between church and world; it is because of its ministry to the person that the church is engaged in enhancing the moral and material conditions of the world. Anthropology leads therefore to ecclesiology: the church's work in the world is at one level a response to the concrete needs of the person. Ecclesiology is tied to eschatology: the church responds to the needs of the person in the first instance because of the intrinsic moral value of meeting human needs, but the work of the church in the world has eternal meaning and value; it prepares for the kingdom. Finally a strong christological theme ties anthropology, ecclesiology and eschatology together; each of the four chapters of Part I concludes with a christological summary.

The rich theological argument of *Gaudium et Spes* brings the earlier theological work of de Lubac, Congar et al. to a new level of integration, and with new authority in the Catholic tradition. The principal achievement of the text was to provide a new basis for Catholic social teaching and social ministry. By rooting them in the service of the person and showing this ministry's relationship to the eschaton, Vatican II provided a rationale for the church's engagement in the world which was previously lacking. A second value was the subordination of the classical church-state questions to the broader apostolic conception of the church as a servant in the world. The institutional questions of relationships with the state and other secular entities retain a crucial importance, but they are couched in a broader vision of ministry.

The consequences of *Gaudium et Spes* in the church are best evaluated at two levels in the life of post-conciliar Catholicism. First, the record of Catholic engagement with the world in defense of human dignity and in support of human rights, in public advocacy for peace and in support of social justice demands a systematic explanation. While this kind of secular engagement is hardly new with Vatican II, there has been a pattern of Catholic activism in diverse political and cultural settings which points toward a common source. The ecclesiological significance attributed to serving and shaping the world by *Gaudium et Spes* provides an authoritative impetus for such activity, giving it a substantive theological basis. This theological rationale, ecclesial and eschatological, has provided the basic motivation and even methods of ministry for the church in Latin

America, the Philippines, Central Europe, South Africa and the United States. A Catholic "activism" with solid theological credentials has been the signature of post-conciliar Catholicism.

Second, *Gaudium et Spes* has catalyzed distinctive theological movements since 1965. While both the Theology of Liberation and Political Theology move beyond the conciliar text, they reflect methodological and substantive themes found in it. In a more detailed treatment one could both find the lines of continuity from the council to post-conciliar theologies, and specify the distinctive contributions which such theological reflection has added to the conciliar vision.

Church and World: Contemporary Issues

In the United States the impact of *Gaudium et Spes* was clearly evident in the pastoral letters of the 1980s on nuclear policy and the economy. In both instances the teaching of the bishops *extended* the style and substance of *Gaudium et Spes* to the setting of one "local church." Unlike Political Theology in Europe or the Theology of Liberation in Latin America, the church in the United States has produced less a distinctive school of theology than a linear elaboration of the conciliar vision.

In closing I seek to provide a sense of how that extension of *Gaudium et Spes* takes shape in the world on a range of issues. The goal here is not an in-depth analysis of any issue, but an illustration of how the Catholic conception of church/world/society yields a position on specific topics.

In foreign policy the core Catholic concept is the unity of the human family, based on common origin, common nature and common destiny. Sustaining this idea are the theological doctrines of creation and eschatology as well as the philosophical premise of a natural law ethic. This idea of the unity of the human community was central to de Lubac's *Catholicism* as well as to Augustine, Aquinas and the Spanish Scholastics (Vitoria and Suarez). In the structure of Catholic teaching on international relations, the unity of the human community is the master concept for the following more specific themes.

In twentieth-century papal teaching on international relations, the basic structure posits the existence of a human community, united by moral bonds of rights and duties, but lacking an adequate legal, political and economic structure to achieve its destiny. Pius XII articulated the basic lines of this argument which has since then been developed politically by John XXIII in *Pacem In Terris* (1963) and economically by Paul VI in *Populorum Progressio* (1967) and by John Paul II in his human rights address to the United Nations (1979). Flowing from this basic structure is Catholic teaching on the status of the nation-state; the state has clear moral standing but its role is relativized by the pre-existing moral obligations which unite and bind all persons. Such a view of the nation state, which sets clear moral limits on its claims and its power, establishes the basis for Catholic teaching on war (a *limited* right of defense exists) and its teaching on economics (both individuals and states bear responsibilities for policies affecting economic justice at the global level).

In brief, Catholic teaching on international relations affirms a moral structure for the world which goes quite beyond any existing political framework, but which arises directly from de Lubac's conception of "the corporate destiny" of the human community.

In terms of U.S. foreign policy in the 1990s, the premises (and, to be honest, the tensions) of Catholic teaching are evident when confronting the issue of military intervention. In the secular political debate, the norm of nonintervention, which has been in possession politically and legally for three hundred years, is now under pressure and under review. Proposals are advanced from several sources to rethink and to relativize the nonintervention norm in the name of protecting human rights and quelling civil conflicts which threaten entire societies like Bosnia and Rwanda. The logic of Catholic teaching, rooted in human unity, has always been at odds with an absolute conception of nonintervention. Some forms of military intervention have been understood as obligations of human solidarity.

The tension in contemporary Catholic teaching arises because the ethic of war has grown increasingly restrictive in light of the destructive capabilities of modern warfare. The Catholic ethic of intervention seeks to reconcile an expansive conception of transnational moral responsibility with a very narrow conception of when force can be used as an instrument of policy. In the context of the contemporary U.S. policy debate, the Catholic position both presses the case for engagement and sets rigorous standards of limits in fulfilling the engagement.

On a quite different front, Catholic teaching on bioethics also exemplifies its conception of church-world engagement. Here the controlling concepts are the sacredness of life and the notion of stewardship. The sacredness of every person is the foundational idea for Catholic political ethics and for bioethics. The defense of the person, in John Courtney Murray's words, is the *locus standi* for the church in the world, its point of entry to the political order and its rationale for social engagement.[19] The concept of sacredness leads directly to the principle of stewardship, the idea that both positive duties and decisive restraints govern the "taking" or the "touching" of human life. This double moral agenda, for *care* of human life and for *restraint* in the exercise of care undergirds Catholic teaching in *Donum Vitae* (1987) and *Evangelium Vitae* (1995). The stewardship principle governs both texts, affirming a right and responsibility for science and medicine to explore the range of therapeutic measures which can enhance and extend human life, while asserting firm prohibitions against abortion, euthanasia, and experimentation with fetal life. Catholic bioethics is shaped by themes which are central to the church-world question: responsibility for the world, exercised through research and technological innovation; conviction about the social nature of the person which in turn sets the context for assessing issues of bioethics from a social perspective; a sense of the real but limited nature of human responsibility (that of creatures not the creator) which is shaped by an understanding of history and eschatology.

The product of these themes is an ethic for medicine and the life sciences which is neither passive in terms of human responsibility nor willing simply to affirm human autonomy in the face of issues of life and death. Like the ethic of intervention Catholic bioethics is in tension, affirming broad responsibilities for the world, but interpreting responsibility in precisely defined categories.

A similar tension marks the Catholic ethic of the state. While church-state relations are subordinated to the wider church-world issues by *Gaudium et Spes*, the institution of the state uniquely represents challenges posed for the church by the world. The research of Congar and Murray helped Catholicism to affirm the secularity of the state as a good while still maintaining a double restraint on state power. The state was "relativized" by measuring its temporal role against another more lasting "city" as Augustine did; the state was also "limited" in history by the claims of a specific institution, the church.

These restraints on the power of the state did not seek to produce, however, a doctrine of the minimalist state. In fact Catholic teaching prescribes for the state a broad range of moral responsibilities, articulated in terms of its teaching on human rights and social justice. The tension of the Catholic ethic of the state is embodied in its support for the subsidiarity principle (restraining resort to state power) and its support for the view that the state is not simply an instrument of order, but an active moral agent in pursuit of the common good for all.

Each of these issues, at the heart of the U.S. policy debate today in terms of Bosnia, abortion and euthanasia, and budgets and social policy, requires a lecture to show how the tensions of the Catholic ethic are worked out in detail in a church-world dialogue. My more limited purpose has been to show how the macro-categories of church-world theology take shape in a Catholic social ethic which engages the world, seeking to collaborate in building a society "which even now is able to give some kind of foreshadowing of the new age."

Thirty years ago *Gaudium et Spes* opened a new chapter in the long history of the church-world question, urging Catholics to use the resources of faith and reason to reflect the new age even now in this age of history. It is essential to the purposes of Catholic higher education to assist the church in responding to the world in all its complexity and challenge. The opportunity and the obligation to do so for the church in the United States are measured by the evident needs of our own society and the inevitable impact the United States has on the world. It has been a privilege to use the Marianist Lecture to renew the call of the council, and to recognize the gift *Gaudium et Spes* has been to the church and the world in our time.

Notes

1. Gaudium et Spes, in W. M. Abbott, S.J., ed., *The Documents of Vatican II* (New York: Herder and Herder, 1966). Citations will refer to paragraphs in the conciliar text and page numbers in the volume.

2. For most of the major social encyclicals, see D. J. O'Brien and T. A. Shannon, eds., *Catholic Social Thought: The Documentary Heritage* (Maryknoll, NY: Orbis Books, 1992).

3. For an historical and analytical evaluation of developments on church and state see the collection of essays of John Courtney Murray, S.J.: J. Leon Hooper, S.J., ed., *Religious Liberty: Catholic Struggles with Pluralism* (Louisville, KY: Westminster/John Knox Press, 1993).

4. See the assessment of de Lubac's work in: J. A. Komanchak, Theology and Culture at Mid-Century: The Example of Henri de Lubac, *Theological Studies*, 51 (1993) pp. 579–602; also H. Urs von Balthasar, *The Theology of Henri de Lubac: An Overview* (San Francisco, CA: Ignatius Press, 1991).

5. Y. M.-J. Congar, O.P., *A History of Theology* (New York: Doubleday and Company, Inc., 1968) p. 14.

6. Komanchak, cited, p. 593.

7. For background on the broader theological work, cf. Congar, cited; H. de Lubac, *At the Service of the Church: Henri de Lubac Reflects on the Circumstances that Occasioned His Writings* (San Francisco, CA: Ignatius Press, 1993) pp. 60–96.

8. H. de Lubac, *Catholicism: A Study of the Corporate Destiny of Mankind* (New York: Sheed and Ward, 1958) p. x.

9. *Ibid.*, p. 19.

10. Gaudium et Spes, #1, pp. 199–200.

11. Y. M.-J. Congar, *Lay People in the Church: A Study for a Theology of the Laity* (Westminster, MD: Newman Press, 1957) p. 78.

12. *Ibid.*, p. 81.

13. *Ibid.*, p. 91.

14. J. C. Murray, On the Structure of the Church-State Problem, in W. Gurian and M. A. Fitzsimmons, eds., *The Catholic Church in World Affairs* (Notre Dame, IN: University of Notre Dame Press, 1954) pp. 11–32.

15. J. C. Murray, The Issue of Church and State at Vatican Council II, in L. Hooper, cited, pp. 199–228.

16. Y. M.-J. Congar, The Role of the Church in the Modern World (Part I, Ch. 4) in H. Vorgrimler, ed., *Commentary on the Documents of Vatican II* (Freiburg: Herder, 1969) vol. V, p. 220.

17. Gaudium et Spes, #39, p. 237.

18. Congar, The Role of the Church, cited, p. 208.

19. Murray, The Issue of Church and State, cited, p. 220.

About the Authors

SIDNEY CALLAHAN is a Professor of Psychology at Mercy College, Dobbs Ferry, N.Y., and Georgetown University. She received her B.A. from Bryn Mawr College, an M.A. in psychology from Sarah Lawrence, and her Ph.D. in social psychology from the City University of New York in 1980. She is licensed as a psychologist by the state of New York.

Dr. Callahan is the author or editor of nine books. They include *In Good Conscience: Reason and Emotion in Moral Decisionmaking; With All Our Heart and Mind: The Spiritual Works of Mercy in a Psychological Age; Abortion: Understanding Differences;* and *Parents Forever: You and Your Adult Children.* She has published over 200 articles and essays in such publications as *The New Republic, Concilium,* the *Hastings Center Report,* and *Commonweal.* She writes a regular column on medical ethics for *Health Progress,* is a columnist for *Commonweal,* and has appeared on the Today Show, the McNeil-Lehrer Hour, and Firing Line, among others.

Sidney Callahan has lectured at over 300 American, Canadian, and European universities, and has served as a consultant to the Ford Foundation, the National Science Foundation, the National Endowment for the Humanities, and the Catholic Health Association. She is President of Commonweal Associates, and Chairperson of the Board of the Catholic Commission on Intellectual and Cultural Affairs, and the Association for Rights of Catholics in the Church.

121

Dr. Callahan is married to Daniel Callahan, co-founder and Director of The Hastings Center. They are the parents of six adult children.

LOUIS DUPRÉ was born in Belgium and graduated summa cum laude from the University of Louvain with a doctorate in Philosophy. His doctoral dissertation, *The Starting Point of Marxist Philosophy*, was published with a government grant and in 1956 he received the biennial J. M. Huyghe prize in social studies. He came to the United States in 1958 as a professor of philosophy at Georgetown University. In 1973 he was appointed the T. Lawrason Riggs Professor of the Philosophy of Religion at Yale University. He still holds this position at Yale, where he also founded the undergraduate Humanities program.

Professor Dupré is the author or editor of more than a dozen volumes, including *Kierkegaard as Theologian, The Philosophical Foundations of Marxism, The Other Dimension, Transcendent Selfhood, A Dubious Heritage, Marx's Social Critique of Culture, Passage to Modernity,* and *Metaphysics and Culture.*

A former president of the Hegel Society of America and the American Catholic Philosophical Association, Louis Dupré has been a visiting professor at the University of Louvain, St. Louis University, Brigham Young University, and the University of California at Santa Barbara and has lectured at many universities in Europe and the United States. He received honorary doctorates from Loyola College (Baltimore), Sacred Heart University (Fairfield), and Georgetown University (Washington, D.C.). In 1995, he was elected a member of the American Academy of Arts and Sciences, and he has been a member of the Belgian Academy since 1985.

JOHN TRACY ELLIS received his bachelor's degree from St. Viator College in 1927, his master's in 1928, and his Ph.D. in 1930 from the Catholic University of America. After teaching history at Viator from 1930 to 1932 and then at the College of St. Teresa of Winona, Minnesota, from 1932 to 1934, he decided to enter the priesthood and completed his seminary studies at the Sulpician Seminary in Washington from 1934 to 1938. He began teaching at the Catholic University of America in 1935 where he remained until 1964. He moved to the University of San Francisco in 1964 and stayed there until 1977, when he returned to the Catholic University in Washington. He published over twenty books, among the best known of which are *The Life of James Cardinal Gibbons* (1952), *American Catholics and the Intellectual Life* (1956), and *American Catholicism* (1956). He received numerous honorary degrees, was a life-long lover of the theater, and commonly considered the dean of historians of American Catholicism. He died in Washington, D.C., in 1992.

PHILIP GLEASON is professor of history at the University of Notre Dame. He was born in Wilmington, Ohio, in 1927 and graduated from the University of Dayton in 1951. After a year as a management intern in Baltimore, and another as an eighth grade teacher in Xenia, Ohio, he embarked upon graduate work in history at Notre Dame, receiving his doctorate in 1960. Except for a term as visiting chaired professor at the Catholic University of America, he has taught at Notre Dame ever since. Professor Gleason also served as chairman of Notre Dame's Department of History from 1971 to 1974, and in 1978 he received the university's annual faculty award.

From 1986 to 1988 Professor Gleason was national chairman of the Catholic Commission on Intellectual and Cultural Affairs. A past president of the American Catholic Historical Association, he has also served as consultant to the Johns Hopkins Program in American Religious History and on the editorial boards of the *Journal of American History* and the *Review of Politics*. He has published many scholarly articles and written or edited seven books, including *Keeping the Faith: American Catholicism Past and Present* (1987) and *Speaking of Diversity: Language and Ethnicity in Twentieth-Century America* (1992). His most recent work, *Contending with Modernity: Catholic Higher Education in the Twentieth Century* (1995), has just appeared.

Professor Gleason is married to Maureen Lacey Gleason who is Deputy Director of the University of Notre Dame Libraries; they are the parents of four adult children.

ROSEMARY HAUGHTON is an internationally known religious scholar, writer, and lecturer. Born in England in 1927 of an

English mother and American father, she is married and the mother of ten children and several foster children, now grown and with families of their own. In 1974 she and her husband and others founded a community in Southwest Scotland, called Lothlorien, which works with mentally troubled people.

Mrs. Haughton began writing in her thirties, and her writing brought invitations to lecture in the United States. Over the years this experience led to her interest and involvement in the movement of Christian communities in North America. She now lives and works in a community whose work developed in response to the needs of homeless people by providing shelter as well as housing, education, family programs, and economic development opportunities for people in poverty in the area. This community, Wellspring House, Inc., in Gloucester, Massachusetts, was founded in 1981 and has gained respect and acclaim for its pioneer work.

In the midst of a life filled with children and service to others, Mrs. Haughton has found the time to write over 30 books. Among her best known books are *The Transformation of Man* (1967 and reprinted 1982); *The Catholic Thing* (1980); *The Passionate God* (1981); *The Re-Creation of Eve* (1985); and *Song in a Strange Land: The Wellspring Story and the Homelessness of Woman* (1990). She has received five honorary degrees and numerous awards for her achievements. She continues to lecture nationwide and to write.

J. Bryan Hehir is the Professor of the Practice in Religion and Society at Harvard Divinity School. With a bachelor's and master's from St. John's Seminary (Boston, Mass.), Fr. Hehir earned a Th.D. in applied theology from the Harvard Divinity School (1977) with specialization in ethics and international politics. Most of his work since taking his Th.D. has focused on his doctoral specialty.

In addition to his present position in the Harvard Divinity School, Hehir is a Faculty Associate in the Harvard Center for International Affairs. Among many posts held prior to taking up his positions at Harvard in 1992, Hehir served as Research Professor of Ethics and International Politics in the School of Foreign Service at Georgetown University, as well as Joseph P.

Kennedy Professor of Christian Ethics in the Kennedy Institute of Ethics, also at Georgetown University. At the U.S. Conference of Bishops, he was director of the Office of International Affairs, Secretary of the Department of Social Development and World Peace, and Counselor for Social Policy.

Fr. Hehir has had a powerful influence on the Catholic Church through his various teachings and administrative posts, but also through such scholarly publications as *The Just-War Ethic Revisited, Christians and New World Disorders, The United States and Human Rights, The U.S. Nuclear Debate: Strategic and Ethical Dimensions, Catholic Teaching and the Church in the Democratic Process,* and *The Church and the Food Crisis.*

Through his articles, his teaching, and administrative positions, as well as his presence on important committees of Catholic bishops in the United States and around the world, Fr. Hehir has profoundly affected the Church's views on war and peace and justice.

For his many achievements, Fr. Hehir has earned two dozen honorary degrees, the Catholic Book Club's Campion Award, the National Catholic Education Association's Albert Koob Award, the Letelier-Moffitt Memorial Human Rights Award from the Institute for Policy Studies, and a MacArthur Foundation Fellowship.

MONIKA K. HELLWIG is the Landegger Distinguished University Professor of Theology at Georgetown University. Born in Silesia in 1929, she grew up there and in the Netherlands, Scotland, and England in the midst of the turmoil of World War II. Her undergraduate and law degrees were from the University of Liverpool, and her M.A. and Ph.D. degrees from the Catholic University of America. She has been a member of the Theology Department of Georgetown since 1967, and has been a visiting summer professor at a dozen universities, including the University of Dayton in 1986.

A past president of the Catholic Theological Society of America, Dr. Hellwig received that society's John Courtney Murray Award in 1984. She is also the recipient of twelve honorary degrees. Among her many professional activities, she has been an associate editor of the *Journal of Ecumenical Studies* since 1973, an editorial consultant for the *Religious Studies Bulletin* since 1983, and was a member of the editorial board of *Theological Studies* from 1981 to 1991. She is a much traveled lecturer and the author of fourteen books and many articles in both professional and general publications. Dr. Hellwig is the single adoptive parent of three now-grown children.

John T. Noonan, Jr. is a judge of the U.S. Court of Appeals, Ninth Circuit (San Francisco). Born in Boston in 1926, he graduated from Harvard and did advanced studies in English Literature at Cambridge University before earning a Ph.D. in Philosophy from the Catholic University of America. He received his law degree from Harvard Law School in 1954. He practiced law in Boston for seven years before joining the faculty of the University of Notre Dame Law School. In 1966 he became professor at the University of California Law School at Berkeley, where he remained until he was appointed a federal judge in 1986.

Judge Noonan is the author of a distinguished list of publications, including these books: *The Scholastic Analysis of Usury; Bribes; Contraception: A History of Its Treatment by the Catholic Theologicans and Canonists; Persons and Masks of the Law; The Antelope; A Private Choice; Power to Dissolve;* and *The Believer and the Powers that Are.* He has a record of wide-ranging service in government, church and academia, and has received eleven honorary degrees, the Christian Culture Medal, the Laetare Medal, and the Edmund Campion Medal, among many other awards.

Judge Noonan is married to Mary Lee Noonan; they are the parents of three adult children.

Timothy O'Meara, an internationally renowned mathematician with interests in modern algebra and the theory of numbers, stepped down as Provost of the University of Notre Dame in June 1996 after a tenure of eighteen years.

A native of South Africa, O'Meara took his baccalaureate and master's degrees from the University of Cape Town and received his Ph.D. from Princeton University in 1953. After teaching at the University of Otago in New Zealand for three years, he returned to Princeton and served on the faculty there between

1957 and 1962. He was also a member of the Institute for Advanced Study in Princeton in 1957 and again in 1962. He joined the Notre Dame faculty in 1962 and fourteen years later was named the Howard J. Kenna Professor of Mathematics. He was appointed Provost in 1978. He has held visiting positions at American, Canadian, and European universities, including the California Institute of Technology, and has held the Carl Friedrich Gauss Professorship at Göttingen University.

From 1960 to 1963, O'Meara was awarded a Sloan Fellowship which he held at Princeton and Notre Dame. He has published numerous research articles and three books, two of which have been translated into Russian. A fourth book, co-authored with Notre Dame colleague Alex Hahn, has been welcomed as the standard reference in its field. As a member of the University of Notre Dame faculty, he twice chaired the Department of Mathematics and served on several key University committees. As Provost, he played a central role in the deliberations that have charted Notre Dame's academic course. In 1991 he was elected a fellow of the prestigious American Academy of Arts & Sciences.

O'Meara was instrumental in establishing a Notre Dame presence in the People's Republic of China during the 1980s. He has also worked with Chinese hierarchy to foster the education of young men and women to aid the church in China. In January of 1996 he and a delegation from the University of Notre Dame visited China to strengthen relationships with Chinese academic institutions, including the Chinese Academy of Sciences.

O'Meara is married to Jean Fadden of Philadelphia, a graduate of Rosemont College and Villanova University. The O'Mearas have five children, all of whom have graduated from the University of Notre Dame.

WALTER J. ONG, S.J. was born in Kansas City, Missouri, and before entering the Jesuits in 1935 he finished his B.A. at Rockhurst College and worked for two years in commercial positions. He did his studies in philosophy and theology (S.T.L.) at Saint Louis University, and earned degrees in English from Saint Louis (M.A.) and Harvard University (Ph.D.). Besides a lengthy teaching career at Saint Louis University, he has held visiting professorships and lectureships at Yale, Oxford, Cornell, Chicago,

Toronto, and other universities. He holds various honorary degrees, one of the most recent from the University of Glasgow (Scotland).

Fr. Ong is University Professor Emeritus of Humanities at Saint Louis University.

A national and international leader in a wide spectrum of intellectual, religious, and cultural organizations, Fr. Ong is well known as a lecturer across the United States and Canada and on national radio and television networks in the U.S. and abroad.

The relationship of rhetoric and culture has been one area of study for Fr. Ong whose research also embraces literature, philosophy, psychology, linguistics, and theology. *Hopkins, the Self, and God,* a book on the English Jesuit poet Gerard Manley Hopkins, is the most recent among his long list of works, which have been translated into French, German, Spanish, Italian, Korean, Japanese, and Swedish.

Fr. Ong was a member of the National Council on the Humanities from 1968 to 1974; served on the White House Task Force on Education in 1967; co-chaired the National Endowment for the Humanities Committee on Science, Technology, and Human Values, and is a fellow of the American Academy of Arts and Sciences.

The brilliance, depth, and breadth of Fr. Ong's contribution to knowledge mark him as one of the foremost scholars in the history of American Catholicism.